Smiling
Through Breast Cancer

*The knot in the pit of my belly for over
20 years prepared me for breast cancer.*

*My smile now shows the joy & exultation in looking past
my pain & allowing God to use me for His glory.*

YVONNE JOYCE DUNKLEY

To order, call 404-452-2225
Visit us at http://www.letsfightbreastcancer.org
Email: info@letsfightbreastcancer.org

Acknowledgements

To my dear loving God, my Papa!

Thank you for allowing your Son, Jesus to guide my path and for the Holy Spirit that stayed with me all the way. I appreciate you for hiking with me throughout my life's journey. We have travelled down some perilous paths together. Lord, even though at times you seemed so far, I just had to trust you still, because I knew it was the plan of the devil to trick me. I will forever trust in you explicitly. As a matter of fact, I will keep my promise in sharing with others of your saving grace to mankind.

You are the all-wise God!

The one who knows my beginning and my end; the one who says that it is not over until I God says so; the one who promises me, *Yvonne, as long as you do not lean unto your own understanding, I will continue to carry you safely.* I love and adore you Lord. You brought me safely to shore riding those tidal waves. You have planted my shaken feet on solid ground and you have strengthened and calmed my family's worst fears during such turbulent times.
For this I am grateful!

I am looking forward in seeing you on that glorious morning when the dead in Christ shall rise and those who are alive will see you, in your glory.

What a day that will be!

I thank you again Almighty Father for your never-failing, unchanging love towards my family and me.

Your loving daughter Yvonne!

DEDICATION

This book is dedicated to the memories of my parents

Albertha Headley, affectionately called Mavis and

Allan Headley, affectionately called Deacon.

You loved me and cared for me as a child. I then grew into a young lady, got married and you showered my family and me immensely with total, unconditional love.

You both are gone, but the seeds you have planted in your loving grandchildren, my wonderful husband and me, have been an everlasting guide in our lives, as we go throughout life's journey today.

Rest in peace until that glorious day when we will meet on that beautiful shore.

THE DUNKLEY FAMILY

The family is God's first institution for man. It was ordained and blessed by Him. This blissful institution has been under attack by Satan from the beginning of time. He will use anyone; do anything and everything to destroy God's handiwork.

"No man hath seen God at any time. If we love one another, God dwells in us and His love is perfected in us." 1 John 4:12

Even though life's journey comes with trials; we will continue to steadfastly hold on to Jesus. Through Him we will victoriously live a happy life because we are still blessed & highly favored by our Heavenly Father!

To my loving, caring husband
Colin Dunkley

I will never forget twenty years ago when outside influences tried to crumble our world and you told me, "Yvonne, I don't know my father, he was never there for me. I will never forsake or leave my children. I want them not to see me as a father, but a Dad.
I love you and if you hang in there with me we can make it together".

Two years ago, we found ourselves facing my breast cancer. Again, you told me, "Yvonne, the Lord will not give us more than we can bear and I will be there for you always".

Colin, when you shaved your head because you wanted to share my bumpy, rocky breast cancer journey; loving me at my most unattractive, vulnerable state (bald head, one breast, black nails etc.) you avowed and affirmed your love for me and our family.

Twenty five years later, here I am medically challenged yet, I feel stronger and even more confident in your warm arms Colin, because you stood by my side. Your love has lifted me higher above any trials that came to test us. Just look at us now, swinging 'hand in hand', empowering other families. We are wiser, stronger and more in love.

You are truly my precious jewel that lights up my mornings; that shines brightly throughout my days; and that soothes my nights especially in difficult times.

You are my soul mate!

For that Colin, I give God all the praise!

My children

Tanya, Chadeesia, Coleen & Yvonna

I could not have asked God for better children. I am so thankful to the Almighty Father for the wonderful, supportive and kind children in my life. I could not have made it this far without your unconditional love and patience. With God in our vessel we will forever stay unbreakable.

A home that prays together stays together.

This book is also dedicated to you all.

Your loving mother!

I would like to thank Dr. Cheryl Samuel and Cimone Brown for their overwhelming support and Sis Sherolin Daley for her spiritual guidance throughout this project. I thank Melissa Bonnick-Anderson for undergoing the task of helping to edit the book as there was so much I wanted to say!

Foreword

When I received a call from Yvonne, I had no idea what it was about. She was full of joy as always. The conversation started with the usual pleasantries then she said, "Girl, I have something fi (to) tell yuh (you)" in her delightful Jamaican accent. Then with her usual lively voice she said, "They tell me I have breast cancer!" I said "What!!!" She continued to laugh and I choked up... "Are you serious?" I think at that point I was more ready to pass out while she continued to laugh and talk, as though she hadn't just imparted devastating news.

I was speechless and she kept asking, "Are you there and are you okay?" I couldn't speak, because in my mind the only thing I immediately heard was, "I am dying." She eventually tried to calm me down by telling me "nuh (do not) worry, God is able," but all I could say was, "I will call you back". From my frame of reference, being a nurse for over twenty years, having seen many folks go through the experiences of cancer, and having just lost my aunt prior to the news, the only thing I could think was "Here we go again," another person to vomit and wither away, until she dies. Also, I thought she was really crazy for reacting that way. It took me several days before I could call back. In fact she called me back to see if I was doing okay.

Yvonne definitely defied all odds; proving that a bald head could be fashionable; that a flat chest could be fun; and this was a way to lose the extra pounds she always wanted to get rid of. She definitely took all her obstacles and turned them into stepping stones. Nicknamed "Mad-Lyn" by my husband, we thought that this laughing, vibrant, victorious person with a joyful approach about everything that she did or was challenged by, could only be totally mad or insane. I applaud Yvonne for her effortless display of positivity and valor in the face of desperation, illness, and death. She chose to tread the "narrow path" of praise and celebration rather than gloom and despair. She has overcome. Her definition of faith and her belief in God is as no other person I know. She is evidence that if we allow God to direct our path, we don't need any other telling.   - Althea Mills (MSN)

Preface

My name is Yvonne Headley-Dunkley and the Lord used the 'thorn in my flesh' to prepare me for breast cancer. My early life's struggles crippled me mentally, physically and spiritually. It made me wonder why life was so cruel. As I grew older and more experienced in my relationship with Christ; I became more at peace with life as I understood that there will always be turbulences in this world.

As long as I stand on the premise of God's promise, I can surmount any obstacle. Now, I realize I was never a victim. I am a victor. I choose to use my mess as a message to minister to women. So, I will delight myself in the Lord and stay on cloud nine while the storms of life rage. Trouble will come, but how I choose to react, will determine the outcome. I will surf the waves and I will use my trials for the good of others and allow them to bring me closer to my Lord as I look to him for guidance.

I wrote this book to inspire, encourage and to remind us of God's everlasting love!

I presently live in a suburb of Atlanta, Georgia with my four beautiful daughters and wonderful husband. I am a Breast Cancer Survivor for the past two years. I was born, educated and raised as a Seventh-day Adventist. While I was sick, I told the Lord if he made me well again, I would dedicate the rest of my life to sharing the wonderful words of his saving grace.

Long before I was afflicted by this dreadful disease, I had a wonderful childhood. I did not know that I grew up poor, because I never defined myself by possessions, which is why I now appreciate everything I have. I believe that in every experience, the Lord can use us as a conduit to spread his loving words to the world. We have the option of seeing our challenges in a positive or negative light. We can either look at the cup as half full or half empty. Even though this awful disease left me medically challenged, I wish to consider my blessing as a cup full and running over. And on this note, I am sharing my life story with you.

Although we find several noble women in the Bible, the details of their stories were never told. I want to share a modern-day story of how my journey has transformed me from tragedy to triumph, victim to victor; how the power of God marvelously worked in my life to make me a conqueror and a crusader; an advocate and an activist for Breast Cancer Awareness. I want to share how over twenty years of experience anchored and moored my soul in a man called Jesus. I want to share how I have become a wonderful support and example for my four children.

My daughter once said to me, "You are my hero. I could not have survived such a prognosis..."

I am here to let the world know that with God in the vessel, you can smile at any storm. You can ride on your waves and rest assured God will take you to shore safely under His wings.

I believe there are three things that impact a person's life: God, heredity, and environment. I want to show my readers where I was at age 21, and where I am now at age 48. I want to show you that through the power of God, you can prevail over and withstand anything. When I look at how the stories of Job and David in the Bible are able to motivate people today, I am convinced that my story will bring hope, revitalize, uplift, and draw souls to Christ.

I am the last of eight children. My mother had me at age 45. I was born on November 1, 1964 in the friendly tourist attraction city, Montego Bay, Jamaica. In those days, society looked down on women having children late in life. I was born from a special person. My mother was a strong, hardworking, and resilient black woman with little or no education. She left Stonehenge, St. James, where she was born and at the age of fifteen, she moved to the big city of Montego Bay, where she did housekeeping.

Striving for more and working within her limitations, my mother became a successful entrepreneur. She walked door to door selling clothes from a suitcase. She was the best "unschooled" mathematician I knew. No one could rob her even though she wrote no figures down and computed everything mentally. Her communication skills were above par and she was very intuitive. She was an excellent salesperson. My mother knew how to stretch a buck and still end up with a buck and a half. Most importantly, she imparted to her children the need to be honest, recognizing that no man is an island. Above all, she put God first in her life.

When my mother had four children, her philosophy was, "better to have loved and lost than never to have loved at all." Not giving up on love, she hoped for God to send her a knight in shining armor. She always saw the cup as half full.

Years later, she met my father and had four more children with him. My father, on the other hand, was cool as a cucumber; a supporter and provider. A builder by trade, he was always like a lion guarding and shielding his pride. He took pride in a job well done, one of the many traits he passed on to his children.

My father took care of his children, so I knew what to expect in a man. My parents adored and cared for their grandchildren. It was always a pleasure for them to have the grandchildren.

My mother was the matriarch in the family. She had taken care of many children: her eight and my sister Carmen's children while she was in her fifties. My sister Pauline was killed by her husband in Canada, leaving behind her two sons Orrette and Oneil. My mother raised them while in her sixties. When I was going through my family struggles, she took my three children while in her seventies. I truly believe God held my parents together so they could impact the lives of their grandchildren. My mother was the original "cougar"; my father was ten years her junior, yet they lived fifty loving, rich, and fulfilling years together.

During the last five years of my mother's life, she could not walk. She was blind in one eye and barely saw out of the other. Also, she had Alzheimer's, high blood pressure, diabetes, and was bed ridden. Thank God, I had the resources to go home and visit her once every three months. My mother passed away in 2005 at the age of 85 and my father died in 2009. They lived a rich and fulfilled life.

I lift my hat to them both. We surely miss them; gone but not forgotten.

Rest in peace!

Table of Contents

CHAPTER 1

The Diagnosis

On Thursday, April 29, 2010, I was diagnosed with HER2-negative breast cancer. This form of cancer is estrogen (hormone)-driven. Hearing the devastating news left me numb and in shock. I could not believe that someone as vibrant and energetic as me could have breast cancer. The news came at a time in my life when the United States of America's economy had taken a nose dive and I had gone to school to reinvent myself. It was two weeks into final examinations for all the colleges, including mine. My daughters, Chadeesia and Tanya, were finishing up nursing school.

Mammogram

On Thursday, April 22, 2010, I went in for a routine mammogram. I had no idea the result would change my life forever. After the technician placed my breast on the machine, I noticed two minutes into the procedure her facial expression was changing. I proceeded to ask, what was wrong; she then asked me to have a seat inside the waiting room and that she would be back. She came out to the waiting room after looking at the film and told me she needed more shots. At that time, I started to feel nervous and anxious. She took me back to the examination room and I started to panic. After doing one round on the machine she told me I was too tense hence, she was not getting the position she wanted. At that moment, I asked her for a minute to pray. I closed my eyes and started to pray. I said, "*Lord, Jesus I am not feeling good and I am asking you to be near at this moment. I don't know what lies ahead of me, but I know you know so come near by my side and watch over me.*" After the prayer, I told her she could start again.

During this time, I kept my eyes closed with this song on my mind.

"*The blood that Jesus shed for me, way back on Calvary, It's that blood that gives me strength from day to day, and it will never lose its power*".

And as I sang this song, I started to feel lighter and I could feel my entire body relaxing. In a second, she said, "I think I got a good shot". She then asked me to go back to the waiting room until someone called me. The radiologist came and informed me that they found calcifications in my breast. This is the term they use before the biopsy confirms cancer.

There were no open appointments for that day. So, they asked me to come in on Tuesday. I got up from the chair in the radiologist's room in a state of frenzy and hysterics. I remember feeling weak inside. On my way home I could hear a voice saying in my head, "you are going to die". There is no way out, because you have cancer. I tried to force myself to sing a song in order to soothe my mind, but it was as if the voice was drowning out the song. With a loud shout, I asked the Lord to show Himself right then. I needed him now, not yesterday, not tomorrow, but now. Right away! Upon reaching home, I sat the children down to let them know what the radiologist told me. They all were terrified and scared. In a state of turmoil, each day seemed so long, as though it was a year. I could not wait for Tuesday to come.

Biopsy

On Tuesday April 27, 2010, I could not even wait for the time of the biopsy appointment to come. I got dressed hurriedly, slipped out of the house without anyone noticing me and showed up an hour before the appointment. After an hour of waiting, my name was called. The routine was the usual, "Take off your clothes in the dressing room, put one of the hospital gowns on and fill out a short form." About five minutes after changing, the doctor called me in. She then sat me in front of this machine, placed my breast between the two glass plates, and proceeded to take out a three inch long needle to biopsy the area where they had found calcification. I was about to scream when the nurse asked me to close my eyes or turn my face away from the procedure. I believe they anesthetized the area, because I really did not feel the needle being inserted into my breast. After the procedure, I was cleaned up by the nurse because I was bleeding a little. Then I was told to come back the next two days for the result. In moments like these, I believe it is the unknown that kills us.

Biopsy Result

In spite of the mental torture I was going through for the next two days, I kept telling myself, God is in control of everything and he would not take me this far to leave me alone. Hastily, again on Thursday morning, April 29, I found myself at the doctor's office to receive the results. I was hopeful that I did not have cancer. As I sat down, the doctor was trying to find a nice way to break the news to me, but with my knees shaking and my mind racing, I blurted out, "Do I have cancer or what?" She slowly confirmed my worst fear.

It seemed surreal. I was wondering how someone as bubbly, vivacious, and bouncy as me could have breast cancer. Someone as energetic and with so much life cannot have breast cancer. In a state of shock, I started to feel weak, drained, and flushed. The doctor asked me if I was okay. I ignored the question, because it seemed as if she expected me to be jumping for joy instead of facing this darkness. I remembered her giving me two prescriptions and me asking what they were for. She told me that one was for the surgeon and the other was for the pharmacy. I then asked what the medication was for and she told me it was for my nerves. Right there and then she was telling me, the road from here is going to be a rough path.

The storm had begun to rage. I ran out of the doctor's office, got into my car not knowing how I got through several red lights. All I remembered was me screaming out to the Lord, saying, "*Lord, My storm is about to start. I do not know how to go through it. I need your help*". I told Satan that he was only driving me closer to God and I probably needed this moment, because I know without a doubt this was not God's doing!

James 1:13 says, "*When under trial, let no one say: 'I am being tried by God.' For with evil things God cannot be tried nor does he himself try anyone.*"

I told God not to give up on me now, because I was not about to give up on him. I decided right there and then that I was not going to be bitter through my storm, I was going to be better; I was going to allow God to give me a makeover; one with a new heart and spirit, a heart like His. I elected not to ask God, "Why me?" I knew the God I serve favored me. After getting home from the doctor, I broke the news to my husband and my girls. They were devastated. We cried and cried and cried. My children reassured me that they had my back and my husband told me that the Lord would not give us more than we could bear, and that he would be there for me always.

For the next few days, as a family, we tried to compose ourselves, grasping at straws with one determination to challenge God. We then turned to the internet, 'Googling' God's promises to us. My husband came up with:

1Corinthians 10:13- *"No temptation has seized you except what is common to man. And God is faithful; he will not let you be tempted beyond what you can bear. But when you are tempted, he will also provide a way out so that you can stand up under it".*

Isaiah 26:3-*"Thou wilt keep him in perfect peace, whose mind is stayed on thee: because he trusted in thee."*

We were confirmed that we were safe as long as we keep God as the center in our lives.

I was brought up in the Seventh-day Adventist faith and I reminded my family to look to God for direction, knowing his promises are firm, sure and reliable. As painful and weak as I felt, I decided to anchor my trust in God. As humans we tend to fear anything that we know nothing about. We love to be in control of our families and surroundings. Sometimes our fear mechanism helps protect us from dangerous situations. Nevertheless, I decided to take this issue of breast cancer by the horns with confidence that as long as I have Jesus Christ in my corner I would be triumphant.

Not knowing much about cancer and wanting to know more about it, I began doing my own research with the aid of my laptop. The best website I found that explained this disease satisfactorily was:

http://www.mayoclinic.com/health/breast-cancer/HQ00348

"Cancer develops when cells in a part of the body begin to grow out of control. Although there are many kinds of cancer, they all start because of uncontrolled growth of abnormal cells."

"According to the Centers for Disease Control, breast cancer is the most common cancer diagnosed in women in the United States. It is the second leading cause of death after lung cancer. Incidence increases with age and all women are at risk."

According to the www.mayoclinic.com, there are two types of breast cancer:

"Noninvasive (in situ) breast cancer: In situ breast cancer refers to cancer in which the cells have remained within their place of origin — they have not spread to breast tissue around the duct or lobule.

Invasive breast cancer: Invasive (infiltrating) breast cancers spread outside the membrane that lines a duct or lobule, invading the surrounding tissues. The cancer cells can then travel to other parts of your body, such as the lymph nodes." (www.mayoclinic.com)

Consulting with the Surgeon

On May 5th, 2010, I went for my first consultation with the many doctors in the cancer arena to decide my fate. After sitting with the surgeon, my treatment plan emerged. It was to surgically remove the entire breast (mastectomy), which would remove all the breast tissue, along with any infected lymph nodes in the armpit if there were any.

I was overwhelmed with all the information after listening to the surgeon. The part of my anatomy that defined my femininity was going to be cut off. I remembered the day I got my first bra. I could not wait, because I was a late bloomer. I was one of the happiest people in the world and I felt like a woman. I breastfed my children with them and they were part of my love life. Now, I had to cut them off. A decision to be made in the space of a minute about something I have had for over thirty-five years. But then I heard God reminding me that in Matthew 5:29:

"If your right eye causes you to sin, gouge it out and throw it away. It is better for you to lose one part of your body than for your whole body to be thrown into hell"

So, I opted to remove my breast and tried to keep my mind on the little glimmer of hope from the doctor when she said she would refer me to a plastic surgeon, who would give me a new breast. The plastic surgeon would take the muscle from my stomach to make the breast, so I would even have a tummy tuck. All this information was new to me and it was said so casually that I did not know how to digest it... but the tummy tuck sounded good.

After leaving the surgeon's office, I went outside to get some fresh air. The sun was shining and I raised my two hands toward heaven and with a holler, I said, "Satan, you lose!" While the tears were running from my eyes, I proclaimed my father's words according to 1 John 4:4.

"Greater is he that is in me than he that is in the world". God is my rock and God alone!"

The surgeon wanted to operate the following day, but I could not do it then. My daughter Chadeesia was graduating with her Bachelor of Science in Nursing. I had to see her receive her degree, because I had waited so long to see that day. I talked with God about my children and I decided not to worry and to allow God to continue to work in my life.

CHAPTER 2

My Journey through Treatment

Mastectomy

After I had consulted with several doctors in the breast cancer arena, my brothers Peter and Paul and their families came to visit from New York. I used the time to reassure myself and my family, knowing that God would take us through this.

On Thursday the 6th of May, I went in to be registered in the hospital for my mastectomy surgery. I was first sent to a lady in a cute little booth where she asked me for my insurance and identification cards. She then asked me for the deductible/co-payment which came to over two thousand dollars. This was the first time it dawned on me that there was a major expense attached to this disease. I thought to myself, "I have to cover the other 20 percent as a deductible!" Now let me put this in perspective.

I was mentally concentrating on my breast being cut off and my mind was absorbed by the unknown as I wondered whether the surgery was going to be a success. I did not give any thought to the money to be paid for the surgery and so when I heard this; it was almost like a blow to my system. This was a Thursday and my husband was not getting paid until the next day, which meant the cash would not be available until Monday. I did not know that I was supposed to pay over two thousand dollars that morning at registration; but as usual my God came through for me and sent me to the right person. I ended up telling this person my whole sorry story and thank God she was compassionate and kind. The woman looked at me and said, "Lady, do you have even a hundred dollars?"

I ended up writing a check for a hundred dollars (even though I had no money in my account at the time). So all I could do was pray that they did not present the check to the bank before then... I know that God put her there for me. This is why my faith is so strong. God walks right beside me every step of the way.

Now if this should happen to you or if you know of anyone in the situation I was in, please do not let the financing deter you from getting help. Help is out there. Do your homework and have some faith that God will always come through for you if you ask Him to.

2 Timothy 1:7-"*For God has not given us the spirit of fear; but of power, and of love, and of a sound mind*"

After registering, I went home to pray, read the Bible and get comfortable. I needed the time to focus on my daughter's graduation service and graduation party, which would allow me to be on a euphoric high, and add to my mental fortitude. That night I gathered all the necessary things I needed for the party. I literally forced myself to think above and beyond my situation and be positive, because I had a graduation to attend and a party to host. Believe me, this was a time that I knew my past helped me to cope with my condition. I remembered in my past, how I struggled mentally with my external influences and still had to be strong for the children and my husband. This courage and resilient attitude could only come from God.

On Sabbath morning I got up early as usual, prepared a big breakfast, got my foster son's church suit out, and finished the rest of the food for the graduation party. The graduation was at 10 am and the graduation ceremony was being held a one and a half hour car ride away from home. So, we got ready and left the house for graduation. On our way to the graduation, my daughter Chadeesia, who had left the house earlier than us called to tell us she forgot her graduation grown at home. On top of all I was emotionally coping with, we told her to go borrow someone's gown, because we were not turning back; we were too close to the school. Luckily, she found someone in the next batch of students graduating at 12:30. The graduation ceremony was great. We took lots of pictures with our family and guests and then headed home where we had a small gathering for Chadeesia.

Before my out of town guests left, they encouraged me to keep my eyes on God. Everyone left the house, leaving only my cousin Donna from Florida. The party was finished and all the excitement was done. My brain quickly switched off from the party to my dark, gloomy world where only Jesus could help me. I had to pick up the pieces of my worst nightmare, breast cancer. This was a time I used to encourage myself by praying to the everlasting Father above for guidance and deliverance from this frightful disease. I prayed, I prayed, and I prayed. In light of all the news from the doctors, I felt I still needed more information. I believe lack of information is a source of stress even more so than the ailment. My mind was racing like a computer; my body was feeling shaky again, and I wanted to know more about life and death.

Death is a topic people do not like to talk about, but I wanted to know more. I got my Bible, went to the basement where it was noiseless and peaceful and researched my Bible.

1 Thessalonians 4:16-18
"For the Lord, Himself will descend from heaven with a cry of command, with the voice of an archangel, and with the sound of the trumpet of God. And the dead in Christ will rise first. Then we who are alive, who are left, will be caught up together with them in the clouds to meet the Lord in the air, and so we will always be with the Lord. Therefore encourage one another with these words."

1 Thessalonians 5:9-10
"For God has not destined us for wrath, but to obtain salvation through our Lord Jesus Christ, who died for us so that whether we are awake or asleep we might live with him. Therefore encourage one another and build one another up, just as you are doing."

From studying and reading more, I understood that death is a part of life. Dying in Christ is as if you are sleeping and on that glorious day as long as your loved ones lived and died in Christ, you will see them again. The death and resurrection of Christ gives us hope and eternal life. It gives me confidence that whenever the Lord says my duties are finished on earth, I shall live again in the earth made new. For there is nothing, not even death, that can separate me from the love of Christ.

When I read the story of Hezekiah's illness and how God sent the prophet Isaiah to tell Hezekiah that his time to die had come, and Hezekiah prayed to God telling him all the different reasons why he should live, I was amazed. The Lord granted his wish and gave him fifteen more years of life. However, those fifteen years were terrible as Hezekiah turned from the Lord. And so, I thought that if it was the Lord's will for me to die I would be okay with that. But truthfully, deep down in the human part of my soul I didn't want to die. Like Hezekiah, I started to think of my children. The two eldest ones were less of a worry, because they had careers. The two youngest, Yvonna, had not graduated from Snellville High School and Coleen, from Georgia State University. Even though I contemplated the subject, I believed that I should leave all my worries in God's care; and if He spared my life, I would use the rest of my life to minister about his saving grace.

I began to encourage myself. It is incredible how, with time and experience, one's outlook and attitude toward problems can change. I was no longer the naive 21 year old Yvonne. My past had mentally toughened me up to embrace breast cancer. So, I turned it over totally to God. Without my past, I would not have been mentally and physical ready to face the disaster that had just come into my life. This was when the expression, 'experience teaches wisdom' truly came into play. Recognizing that my heavenly Father came through for me in the past, I had no doubt that he would come through again.

On the Sunday morning of May 16, I received many calls from friends, church brethren, and family members. My cousin Claudette, affectionately known as Donna, fell sick and was admitted in the same hospital I was having surgery in the next day. At about 1 pm, five ladies from the Lithonia Seventh-day Adventist Church came to pray, read, sing, and to anoint me. I was even more assured that my God who died for me had my name right before him.

Surgery

On Monday, May 17, 2010, my entire family took me to the hospital where the nurses prepared me for the operation. I believed wholeheartedly, that my God, my Father, the Chief Surgeon was there ready to cut and remove the infected breast. "Hallelujah!" He was there waiting for me. After many hours, I awakened to see my entire family eagerly waiting to welcome me back. That night my daughter, Coleen stayed with me at the hospital. Chadeesia, the nurse, went to work that night, but was present the next morning to clean me up. She encouraged me to walk that morning, because she said anesthesia slows down the body system. In addition, walking after surgery is crucial in the prevention of blood clots, and enhances breathing.

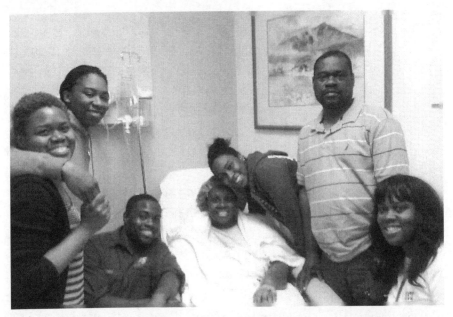

Although my body was protesting, Chadeesia made me walk down the hallway several times. The nurses were happy to see me walking and encouraged me too. That morning the doctor came and was happy, because he got good news from the nurses. So I was discharged the next day leaving my cousin Donna in the hospital.

I went home that day with tubes protruding from every part of my body. Upon my arrival at home, I saw mother Shaw and a family friend Devon leaving my driveway.

When I went inside the house, I saw enough food to feed a multitude. That night, several of the young people from church visited with me. The compassion of these people was such a source of encouragement.

Consulting with the Oncologist

A week after doing my surgery, my surgeon received the Pathology report. She saw the seriousness of my case and referred me to the oncologist. She asked the receptionist of the oncologist for an urgent appointment. On May 26, 2010, not yet recovered, with tubes and bags hanging from my side (to catch all the fluid that my body did not want), my family took me to consult with the oncologist. He informed me that the kind of cancer I had was aggressive and that the pathologist report was showing that the surgeon removed 19 lymph nodes and from those 19, 15 were infected with cancer. So, he recommended six rounds of chemotherapy. He told us, "Chemo is a drug that is given to kill cancer cells and to reduce the high chance of the cancer returning or spreading to another part of my body".

The side effects of chemotherapy would depend on the drugs received. I was given a sheet of paper listing the common side effects, to include hair loss, nausea, vomiting, fatigue, and a small increased risk of developing infection. Also, I was told that I would be given a combination of drugs (Adriamycin, Taxotere, and Cytoxan), which would be injected in my chest through a port connected to my arteries. He then referred me to the radiologist.

Consulting with the Radiologist

Coupled with the oncologist, that day, I sought consultation from the radiologist. She explained that I would be placed inside a high-powered x-ray machine, which would aim energy beams at the part of the body infected with cancer cells, in order to kill them. I would have thirty-five sessions, five times per week. She said that some of the side effects of radiation therapy included fatigue and the area that the beam is radiating may develop in a sore-like sunburn reaction.

Two weeks after all these consultations, my husband took the entire family to Jamaica to recuperate from my mastectomy. My brother Paul and his family were there, also. We had a great time going to the beach, chatting and laughing and eating mangoes, sugar cane, roasted breadfruit, fruit cake, and roasted cod fish and ackee. We enjoyed true Jamaican hospitality. It was both therapeutic and cleansing for my family. This trip rejuvenated our souls after having gone through the horrors of mastectomy.

Chemotherapy

Now, with the help of God, we were mentally and physically prepared to take on step two - the challenges of chemotherapy. When the enjoyment of Jamaica came to an end, I was hastily brought back to reality.

On June 18, I went in to start chemotherapy. Upon arriving at the doctor's office, the nurse asked me what all those people were there for, and why was I smiling like that? Someone in the group said, "We are all here for chemotherapy." The nurse said that she had never seen so many people accompany one person to do chemotherapy. I was led to the room for blood work, then to the doctor's office, where he examined me. After the examination, I went into the chemo room with my family and friends. We sat there for six hours, while three different types of drugs were injected into the port leading to my arteries which would then circulate throughout my body. My support was intact. The support from my family and friends was strong, because they were sent to me from God. What a big difference it makes when you have support. God made such a terrifying, frightening, and distressing moment so easy and comfortable. That is what happens when we trust God and allow him to lead. I wore my smile throughout.

Matthew 17:20 says: "*I say unto you, if you have faith the size of a mustard seed, you will say to this mountain, 'Move from here to there,' and it will move; nothing will be impossible to do.*"

At the start of chemotherapy, the doctors gave me about six prescriptions for nausea and vomiting. Thank God I never took one, because my herbalist introduced me to a book about the healing power of plants and fruits. I read that papaya and pineapple are exceptionally good for digestion.

"*Lord I call you healer; I call you comforter; I call you awesome*".

After my first chemo treatment, the Adriamycin caused me to lose the hair on my head and after the second round my nails became black. During the first seven days of chemo, my body became weak and feeble. My immune system broke down and the doctor gave me an injection called Neulasta two days after chemo. As a result of chemotherapy, I was at high risk for developing infection, because my white blood cell count was low. Chemotherapy hurts the immune system. It lowered my immunity by killing both the good and bad cells that my body produced. White blood cells are important in preventing and fighting infections. I had frequent blood tests during this phase of treatment so the doctor could monitor the levels of different blood cells in the body. If the white blood cell count fell significantly during chemotherapy, it would cause me to be susceptible to infection. This condition is called neutropenia.

I remember the first time my immune system had gotten considerably weak. The nurse forgot to give me Neulasta and my daughter Tanya was very upset with her. I had never seen her like this before. From that day forward, she administered my injection herself.

Neulasta is the drug that was given to stimulate my bone marrow to produce white blood cells that would assist my immune system in fighting off infection during chemotherapy. During my chemotherapy session, my husband would get up at 5:30 am, before catching the bus to go to work, to juice green vegetables and fruits to aid my body with nutrients from green plants. He would call me at least three times during the day, just to perk me up and encourage me. After the second round of chemo, all of my hair fell off my head. It does not matter how much one braces for this experience, it is still a major jolt. I continued my juicing and started to drink Ensure, because by then my taste buds were gone and I had no appetite.

By the third and fourth rounds of chemo I was constantly feeling weaker and more exhausted. I had joint pains which, coupled with my weakness, affected my balance and mobility. I also had rashes in my mouth and my nails were black. Believing that the treatment could not be more unbearable, I moved into the fifth round of chemotherapy. I was mistaken. Being the considerate person he is, my husband called to let me know he was coming to take me out, because he knew I must be having a rough time. So I had to get ready. I got dressed and came downstairs, and my third daughter Coleen wanted to know where I was going so dressed up. I told her that daddy was taking me out. She immediately told me to put a hat on my bald head. My husband was just in time to hear her and he said to her, "If it is okay with Mother, it is okay with me. I have her back"

These words gave me a chill and boosted my self-image as I had been sometimes feeling so un-pretty. Colin helped me to keep my smile through my illness. Even though there were times when I felt as if I was drowning and completely overwhelmed, the Lord was able to keep me in perfect peace. During the days when Adriamycin, Taxotere and Cytoxan almost overpowered me, I found solace and consolation in the book of Psalms. I would read Psalms 27, 37, and 34. Also, I found solace in famous songs on YouTube such as, "I Am Not Alone" by Natalie Grant, "Footprint of Jesus" by Leona Lewis, "Never Would Have Made It" by Marvin Sapp, "The Battle Is Not Mine" by Yolanda Adams, "Stand" by my favorite artist Donnie McClurkin, and many other inspirational songs. Most of all, I found the greatest joy in talking with my Savior Jesus Christ.

On my sixth and final round of chemotherapy, after the routine lab work, doctor exam and getting ready for the actual drugs, the nurse encountered a difficulty with my port. I was sent to the x-ray department where they found that my tube had split from the inside. Satan is evil! He hated seeing me giving my heavenly Father the praise throughout my treatment. They did an emergency operation and took out my port, then gave me a peripherally inserted central catheter line (PICC line) in my left arm. The next day, Friday, I went back and was able to finish my sixth round of chemo. I was able to shout with joy, "*Amen! Amen! Nevertheless thank you Jesus! Thank you Jesus!*"

However, my journey with breast cancer continued to be a really rough road. At moments it seemed like

I couldn't see my way through. But I said, "*Lord, by faith, I am going to hold onto your unchanging hand. My prayer is I need you to clear all the potholes and take me through safely. This is my cry. Lord, dispatch your angels to surround me.*"

By this time my husband shaved his head completely. He wanted to travel the same bumpy road and be in the lane that I was travelling so I would know he was right there for and with me. "*Thank you Jesus for such a caring soul!*" I turned 46 during my final week of chemotherapy, On Saturday, October 31. The treatment broke down my entire body. It made me weak, frail, tired, and made my body susceptible to disease and infection. With each round of chemo I sat for four hours and allowed the doctor to put "poison" into my body. Amazingly, I was happy for this "poison" because it would allow me a little more time in life to see my children "past the worse" as my mom used to say.

As I lay in bed with the full dose of chemo in my body, I felt lifeless, but refused to give up. It was as if the four walls of my bedroom were caving in on me. Trying to find a side to lie on in order to feel comfortable proved futile. As I lay in bed, my mind was racing faster than the fastest man in the world, in the race of his life. My body was aching and I was feeling depressed. In moments like these you feel like there is no hope and no God; but don't I know this is the work of Satan? Well, with most of the hours already gone from the day, tonight was the night I was going to proclaim, broadcast and announce my birthday.

I had no intention of curling up in the fetal position and dying. For too long, Satan had been riding my back. He was trying to weigh me down and drain the life out of me. I called my daughter Coleen with my faded voice and told her to get the camera. While she was getting the camera, I crawled out of bed with my heart beating so fast. Holding on to the furniture, I made my way toward the closet to change out of my pajamas. I found my cream pantsuit that I had not yet worn. It required all I had just to get into it and then painfully, excruciatingly, and agonizingly, I tried to make my way downstairs to pose for the camera.

In my mind I began to argue with myself, heartbreakingly, as I struggled with the part of my mind that was saying, "Go back to bed! At this point of your life you should just give in or give up. Where is your Jesus now?" But I kept ignoring and pushing myself with one determination to reach the living room to pose for my birthday photos. I told myself that tonight, not tomorrow, I will be reaching that mark. I was claiming my birthday that night. I unwaveringly gripped every piece of furniture in my path and made my way to the living room. My sweetie pie daughter, Coleen was there ready and waiting to photograph me that night. As she took the first shot, I told her to let me see it. That picture looked even better than I imagined. This boosted my self-image, my self-esteem, and gave me a better perspective on life. This was one of my chemo triumphs as I trotted on the patchy path of chemo and my God snatched me out of hell's pit.

The more pictures Coleen took, the more my spirit came alive. I was feeling lighter and better and more capable of fighting this disease even though my body was crying out. More than ever I was determined to live. I knew my God had carried me from the valley of death. This was one of my crucial moments, when I established in my mind that I would like to tell the world of how awesome and good my God was to me. I was determined, regardless of what I am going through, I would still trust God and glorify His name. He is worthy to be praised. There is none like Him before, none like Him now, and there will be none like Him in the future. The Muslims call him Allah. The Jews call him Adonay or Elohim, David called Him his Light and Salvation, and I call Him my Healer and Sustainer.

When you have "GOD" you need nothing else in this troublesome world. He is God and God alone!

I posted the pictures on Facebook and my friends were happy to see I was not under the weather. Imagine that! If they only knew! I then called my husband and suggested, "Let's go on a cruise." I was stepping out of my sickness. I refused to let Satan take pleasure in knowing that I was sad and in bed. I was claiming the promises of God. I was going to leave the worries of yesterday, today, and tomorrow to Him. This storm was bigger than I, so I was going to leave it at the foot of the cross and grab my smile back. In the name of Jesus, I was snatching and re-capturing what was mine. My smile! Meanwhile, my Auntie Beverly in Jamaica was praying for me and asking God for the keys of the kingdom of heaven. "Whatever you bind on earth shall have been bound in heaven, and whatever you loose on earth shall have been loosed in heaven." She asked the Lord to bind breast cancer in heaven and on earth and set me free.

As I was going through this rough period of chemotherapy, my adopted mother, Sister Shaw, went with me to check my International Normalized Ratio (INR); because by now, I had a blood clot in my right arm. I remember that morning I did not feel well, but I had to go to the doctor to check my blood so I would know the amount of Coumadin to take for the clot. On arrival at the Lab, there was an emergency situation with another patient so it took far more time for them to attend to me. After what seemed to be an endless wait, I began feeling nauseous.

Eventually, the technician drew my blood; put it into the machine to measure the clot radius among other things. After I was finished, I had to get a new prescription, but the nurse was attending to someone else. Getting frustrated and irritable, I told the nurse to fax the prescription to my pharmacy hoping by the time we got to the pharmacy it would be ready. I struggled to walk to the car with Mother Shaw. When we got to the pharmacy, the prescription was not ready. In fact, the pharmacy had disruptions with their phone line because of a fallen tree. Mother Shaw looked at me with such desperation. I think, as irritable as I was, Mother Shaw was feeling even worse. Needing the medicine so badly, we decided to turn back and drive to the doctor's office to pick up the prescription and take it to the pharmacy.

Since I was feeling extremely ill, she decided to take me home and make me some soup. As soon as she got to her house she dashed inside to make me the soup with some crackers. After that she sent me off to get some rest. There are times when things will never go the way we want them to. This is what life is all about! The Lord did not promise us a bed of roses; everything will not always go the way you want it. Through my experience I have now learned to just raise my hands and ask the Lord for help.

The next visit, I told the doctor of my plan to go on a cruise. I said that I was pronouncing my health. I was taking back my health in the name of Jesus! He ordered a PET scan and was not thrilled about the cruise. He did not recommend such a long trip right now, but since I insisted, he said I would have to check my INR (blood clot) at each port. I called my niece Alethia Miller-Fowler, who is a lab technician in Jamaica, immediately after leaving the doctor's office. "No problem, Auntie Polly. It's done". My appointment was set up at St. Ann's Bay Hospital.

The day before I left for my cruise, I got my lab report and posted this on Facebook:

"Everyone, mercy and grace stopped by my door… got my body scan result today…the doctor found no cancer cells in my body…what did I say people? Grace and mercy stopped by my door…the Lord heard a wretched sinner like me pray. The Lord sees fit to give me one more chance. I am on my way to celebrate my good news on the Carnival cruise. Thank you Jesus!"

My Facebook friends and family were very happy and wished me all the best. We purchased the tickets for the cruise and then left.

I knew that I serve a risen savior, and he was going to take me through. I am truly blessed in every sense of the word. Through my ordeals I kept my smile and found my inner peace.

I made it through Christ and I was going on a cruise to Jamaica, where I could get all my comfort foods such as mangoes, sugar cane, sweet sop, and apples.

Pain should not always be looked upon as a torment, but as something which can be used to propel us forward in our life's journey.

I have learned in my past to look to God when I am in pain. Diamonds are created under much pressure.

Isaiah 43:2 God said, "*When we go through deep waters, he will be with us. When we go through rivers of difficulty, we will not drown. When you walk through the fire of oppression, you will not be burned up; the flames will not consume you.*"

It is through this painful time that God can use us fully. If I did not have sorrow, how would I know to appreciate the good times? It doesn't matter how severe our grief is, we must learn from it. Lean on the Savior. He said, in all things give thanks to God, in the good and the bad times. It is through pain that we will learn to trust and obey the words of God and to build an everlasting friend in him. And most of all, we will grow spiritually. Sometimes we think God is not watching over us. We consider ourselves above the situations; that we don't deserve the pain and that it is unwarranted and too excessive. However, the pain and suffering comes into our lives for a reason. We can give in to the pain or we can stand firm. It is in this special time that God will reveal himself to us. I was determined to live, not die, so I looked to God for that strength.

I read in Exodus 15:2: *"The LORD is my strength and my defense; he has become my salvation. He is my God, and I will praise him, my father's God, and I will exalt him."*

Going through chemo was definitely a challenge; but I realized though things looked discouraging, if I remembered that my strength came from my Heavenly Father and not from myself I was in good hands. The Holy Spirit will supply all the necessary energy to empower me. I have come to understand two words, peace and joy.

Taking Time for Me

Even though my body was weak and frail, I knew God was with me. I needed to remove myself from that atmosphere. I was mentally worn out from the technicians drawing my blood three times a week, the injections from the nurses, the doctors, the children, and dear friends telling me what to do and what not to do. I was bombarded with the task of taking care of myself through chemo. During chemo, I tried not to concentrate on me because that would mean giving in to the pain. I needed to escape from my feelings. So I got out of my skin by reading the Bible, playing motivational songs on YouTube, corresponding with old friends, and meeting new people on Facebook who were just diagnosed with breast cancer. My life consisted of PET scans, CAT scans, X-rays, ultrasound, and sonograms and I was tired! My brain was as exhausted as my body. I needed to take a break so I could regroup. I felt I could only do that far away on the open sea; where it was blissful, calming, and peaceful.

It must be understood that part of the healing process involves getting away from the 'maddening crowd' in order to truly take care of you. It is like a double-edged sword. You need people around you for support, but you need that "me time" for your sanity...that is the balance that needs to be created when going through any issue. My five-day cruise with my husband was just what I needed. It was a relief. I was able to just sit on the deck of the ship, look out on the horizon, and talk with my God. I let him know that I loved him dearly and that He must not give up on me. Oh! How I love him.

While I was on the cruise, Colin wanted to drag me from the room when he wanted to go to a cabaret and I wanted to stay in the cabin and just sleep; while encouraging me that he would be my support and strength. We had started the cruise right after chemo, which meant I was lethargic and lifeless. My body was breaking down from the effects of chemo. Colin would not take 'no' for an answer that night, because he did not want to leave me alone in the room. So I relented and went with him. The funny thing is, I slept throughout the show but I was there and he was with me.

The first port where the ship docked was Ocho Rios, Jamaica. As the doctor ordered, I had to disembark to do my blood work at the nearest hospital. My niece, Alethia Miller-Fowler, had made arrangements at St. Ann's Bay Hospital for me to do my INR. It took just a few minutes and then we were off to enjoy Jamaica. That morning we did not eat breakfast on the ship, because we did not want to spoil our appetite. We found a little hole-in-the-wall restaurant and I had a little cornmeal porridge with a big dish of everything that was on the menu! Everything! All at once, I felt like I was living again. The ship would leave the dock at 4 pm, which meant I had to get my lab report before then. I received the report and called my oncologist and he advised me how to adjust my medicine (Coumadin).

One amazing part of this trip was that when we arrived in Jamaica, even though I was with my husband, the local men were calling out and admiring my bald hairdo. If they only knew it was caused from chemotherapy! After Jamaica, the next port of call was the Cayman Islands. We had a marvelous time. I was still weak, but I would walk then sit periodically. My husband was right beside me, exercising the patience of 'Job'. I thank God for a wonderful man. This goes to show how important the support of a real partner is during a painful and stressful period.

My Side Effects of Chemotherapy

The drugs I received during chemotherapy were Adriamycin, Taxotere, and Cytoxan. These drugs were administered into the body through a surgically implanted port. My port went through my chest cavity to a major artery. They cannot be taken orally and they cannot be injected through a vein, because the medicine is too potent and would burn up the veins. Fortunately for me, I never felt the immediate side effects of nausea and vomiting, because I was counteracting this by taking fruits, such as pineapple and papaya, which are great for digestion. It must be noted that each round of chemo lasted four hours, once every three weeks, over a four-and-a-half-month period—this process was harrowing, because each time my body was built up, only to be broken down by this poison that coursed through me. This is the reason many people do not survive chemo treatment. I thank God every day that I was able to withstand the ravages of chemo. All the praise belongs to Jesus. I could not have done it without Him. For that I owe Him my life.

During the final rounds of chemo, I had a complication with my port. The chemo nurse could not administer the drug because the port had a hole. I had to have an emergency surgery to locate and remove the port that was in my chest. A temporary PICC line was inserted in my left arm, leaving me with a blood clot in that arm. It took over six months to treat the blood clot with the blood thinner, Coumadin. I also had nineteen lymph nodes removed from my right arm. This has left my right arm permanently impaired. I am unable to lift anything over five pounds with this hand. If I do heavy lifting, my right arm can develop lymphedema (fluid retention which leads to swelling of the arm).

In addition, on the entire right side of my body, I have peripheral neuropathy, which is damage of the nerves. This causes my extremities to tingle twenty- four hours a day. A month after chemotherapy, I noticed I had a burning feeling along the side of my legs, but more so the right leg. It was almost like an electric shock or sharp pain on the side of my right leg. I found I could not stand to walk on that leg. My entire right arm, the entire leg and the toes were tingling and I was feeling numbness coupled with memory loss. The severe pain was interrupting my daily schedule and I made an appointment to see my oncologist. After telling the oncologist about my symptoms, he jokingly said to me, "scientists have not come up with any pills for the impaired memory as yet". He went on to tell me about a patient he had who went to the mall and when she was finished shopping she could not find where she had parked her car; so she and the security guard had to wait until the Mall was closed before they could find the car. I couldn't believe it!

He gave me a referral to see a neurologist, who specializes in medical issues related to the nervous system. During the visit, he hooked me up to a machine and attached wires all over my body and pricked me with a needle all over my legs and hands. When he was finished he tried to explain what was going on with my body. He told me that my body is wired with nerve cells called, neurons, axons, and dendrites. The chemo dismantled and disconnected the nerve cells that connected the brain to the spinal cord and throughout the body causing the tingling in my extremities and numbness due to poor circulation. He continued by saying this situation will not get better; it would only get worse over time. He gave me a prescription for Gabapentin 400 mg to be taken 3 times a day for the neuropathy.

The chemotherapy left me with a host of medical issues. I decided to make this my mantra:

To depend on God solely in every aspect of life and in that way whenever the rough times come, I will be able to smile and laugh while the storm of life passes by. I chose to be better, not bitter.

I believe that in order to mentally, physically, and spiritually accept one's cross; Christ has to be the center of one's life. I try to make Him my center in order to bear the cross of breast cancer!

My God is awesome! I made it through chemo and even though I have several medical issues, I am alive. For that I am grateful and thankful. For this, I give God all the praise.

We have an adversary called Satan. His job description is to walk the earth, seeking who he can work through to cause havoc and destroy peoples' lives. He has been roaming earth for many years gathering experience. We as a people who are waiting for the coming of Christ need to be vigilant in our walk, knowing sometimes it is the people who you trust that will let you down. It is the mentors who you have admired all your life who will try to destroy your soul. Even family will dampen your spirit; siblings will dishearten you; your own church family will reject you; but understand and consciously be aware that the God, who died for you and I will never, never go against His words.

Isaiah 46:4 says: *"He will sustain you even when you grow old. This means He will help you withstand any trial, bear any obstacle, tolerate any situation, endure any family issue, and weather any storm as long as you allow him to steer your life."*

We need to travel in faith and hope for the Lord's guidance as we do the necessary things to live a healthy fulfilling life. Prevent stress by doing your annual mammogram to facilitate early detection/diagnosis. Do your Pap smear to test for cervical cancer and test for prostate cancer for men. There are some diseases that can be avoided and early treatment can give you a longer life span.   *Loss Breast wearing Prostisis*

x Breast cancer can leave a woman feeling less than feminine. Having a good self-image is extremely important for the healing of your body. The doctor told me that there are some cases in which a woman goes into total denial. Believing that by losing her breast it means that she is less of a woman. The doctor went on to say that the denial causes them not to seek medical attention immediately. This delay in treatment which permits the tumor to grow faster and bigger and in some cases, the breast actually rots. At this point nothing can be done.

In my situation, before giving my diagnosis, the doctor asked me, "How is your husband going to deal with this?" For some reason that statement did not even register in my brain, because this question was a total non-issue, and had zero relevance at this juncture of my life. If I could not accept me, how could I expect anyone else (meaning my husband) to accept me? If there was one time in my life that I needed to focus on me and my healing, this was it. The lesson here is that anyone suffering from any sickness, especially cancer, needs to understand the concept of "mind over matter". This phrase simply means that one requires mental toughness to battle any terrible illness. At this point, I must state that having spiritual strength is the ultimate weapon. One has to call on God, whoever you conceive Him to be.

Another thing that deters people from seeking help is phobia. The dictionary describes phobia as an irrational fear. It is completely mental and can cripple one's outlook. The ones who suffer from any phobia deal with it from the inside and those looking on from the outside may well describe the person's actions as "stupid." For example, a woman might know that she has full-blown breast cancer and might refuse the mastectomy, because she is afraid of what others might think. That is the worst kind of phobia.

There are many women who refuse to get help, because they think that their partner, whether husband or boyfriend, could not cope with them being without a breast, because they imagine this is their best feature. They would rather die.

I would like to appeal to women living with these phobias that this is your life and this is your body. If you do not take control of it, no one else can. Even if it means going to a psychiatrist to get help, one just has to start somewhere. An irrational fear can kill, and that is what a phobia is.

Similarly, behavioral choices are another issue for women who allow this awful disease to mentally keep them in shock.

Psalm 71:15 *says, "For thou art my hope, O Lord God: thou art my trust from my youth"*

Many women will have the mammogram and mastectomy, complete the treatment, but then, they become paralyzed by the thought of going into public minus a breast. That is crippling fear! This is an aspect of breast cancer that is rarely addressed. A woman spends her life being defined by these two wonderful mammary glands. They fed her children, gave pleasure to her husband and now they are gone. It does create a void in her psyche and requires some mental evaluation to accept.

My advice is to talk, whether to family, friends, or pastors, or anyone who is willing to listen and help. Let them know your feelings. This is not the time to internalize and beat yourself up. This is the time to be grateful and to thank God for being alive.

I personally opted to keep my family and friends involved in all aspects of my care. Cancer does not have to be a death sentence. I did not go to the supermarket and put cancer in my cart; I did not buy breast cancer. I have cancer but it does not define me. I choose to live, not just to exist. I choose to be happy, not sad. I choose to count my blessings, not worries; and I choose to be grateful to God for his saving grace and mercy.

I choose to give God all the glory and keep my smile in my darkest moments, because I know who I serve. I serve a God who told me He is coming back one day for me to live with him forever. In a place where there is no pain or sickness. I serve an all wise God who knows my beginning from my end. Hallelujah!

I admonish anyone who is going through this relentless disease to take that attitude. I can assure you, it will make you feel better about yourself and you will have an appetite for living that will make others wonder.

Radiation Therapy

Step three, which is radiation therapy, is as equally important as chemotherapy. On December 5, 2010, I started my first round of thirty-five rounds of radiation treatment, which burned me up literally. Please don't ignore those annual mammograms and self-examinations. If anyone thinks chemo is bad, I can tell you radiation is worse. I know that, because I went to hell and back. The wonderful thing about it is that I did not stop. The Almighty, Everlasting God carried me through. I thought chemotherapy was horrible losing my hair and all the other terrible things, but now I had to psych myself up for radiation therapy.

Radiation is a different type of treatment. Instead of four hours, I now only had to endure treatment sessions for ten minutes. However, the intensity of these ten minutes was equivalent to four to six hours of chemo. Each morning, I would receive about ten minutes of intense gamma rays. I was instructed to lie on my back in a precise position. I could not move, because the beam was set up to hit an exact location on my right breast where the cancer was found. After about fifteen sessions, the area that was being radiated started to turn black and shriveled like a prune and the skin began to strip away.

In conjunction with the radiation, the doctors recommended that I see a gynecological-oncologist to remove my only remaining estrogen-producing ovary. (Due to fibroids, I underwent a hysterectomy in 2001 and I was left with one ovary.) At this moment I really needed Jesus. When my adopted mother Mrs. Hazel and I arrived at the office for the initial consultation with the gynecological-oncologist, this sweet, kind, and handsome man, who I thought was another patient, sat beside me in the waiting room chit-chatting about whether or not I was comfortable with the proposed procedure. When the nurse called me into the room to wait for the doctor, I got undressed, laid on the bed, and was pleasantly surprised that my waiting room friend was actually the doctor.

Another gift from God! After further discussion, we both decided that I should have the surgery. This estrogen producing ovary was feeding the estrogen based cancer in my breast. It was critical to my ongoing recovery to remove the source of the cancer.

These were necessary but tough decisions for me. In order to survive, I was told that I would have to have more surgery to remove another part of me that defined me as a woman. But through it all, I knew Jesus had a plan for me. As I slowly lost certain aspects of my femininity, if I only trusted in Him, we would make this journey together.

On our way home from the appointment, I had this bright idea for us to take a short cut and not take the route home that Mrs. Hazel knew. I told her to make a right turn, but I used my left hand and pointed to the left. I heard her saying, "which way Yvonne" and again I said turn right, with my left hand gesturing left. With the pressure of the other vehicles behind her and honking horns, she shouted "Yvonne, make your mind up. Is it left or right?"

At that moment, I realized that I was feeling the after effects of the six rounds of chemotherapy and impaired short term memory. We were there on the road and I could not remember which way to go home. We got home safely, but this was just one of those up and down cancer days. I was very happy about the decisions that would move me forward in my healing but at the same time I realized the dramatic changes these decisions would have on my life going forward. This is the give and take of chemo and radiation.

The removal of my ovary was scheduled for a few days after the initial consultation and I felt like I was in a never-ending abyss. I went from checking my INR at 8 am to radiation at 9 am, and to laparoscopic surgery at 11 am, then onto surgery to remove the ovary. It took every ounce of my mental strength and physical fortitude to reach out to touch the hem of Jesus robe for my healing; and it is only by the grace of God that I got through this. My ovary was successfully removed without any complications. "Hallelujah!" The source of my cancer was gone.

Breast cancer allowed me to see the true weakness of man. And on the other, hand allowed me to experience upfront God's true love.

Reflecting on that period in my life, I can truly say, the emotional issues of the previous twenty years prepared me for my battle with breast cancer. The Lord built me up and prepared me for this fight. "Hallelujah!" I literally held onto God's word.

2 Corinthians 12:9 says, "*My grace is sufficient for you Yvonne, for my power is made perfect in your weakness". Therefore I will boast all the more gladly about my weaknesses, so that Christ's power may rest on me"* "*Oh! Thank you Jesus!*"

My dear friend Pauline came down from Canada to help me. I was not yet healed from the ovarian surgery and still doing my INR three times a week. I still had to have twenty more radiation treatments. She took me to each of those sessions taking over the driving duties from Ms. Hazel. By the twenty- fifth session, the first layer of my skin was gone, the area was raw, and heat was emanating from my breast. The doctor told me to put baking soda on it but this only made my situation worse.

One morning during the later stages of radiation treatment, my body was throbbing and aching. I felt as if a truck ran over me. I decided to take a shower and being completely bald I had no need for a shower cap, I stood under the shower and let the water beat down on me from head to toe. I hoped the water would wash off the baking soda from my sore, raw skin. To my surprise it left a white cake-like build up on the affected area. I got out of the shower and sat in front of the mirror. As I stood in front of the mirror and examined my body, all I could see was this big, disgusting circular area with necrotic (dead flesh) tissue at the mastectomy site.

My huge task was to remove the cake-like build up from this huge sore I had developed. My blood ran cold at the mere image of my body, let alone the thought of having to clean off a sore. I reached for my wash cloth and I meticulously and painstakingly wiped away the dead cells and the buildup of the baking soda. Never in my life did I think I would be this disfigured. Looking at the area allowed me to see that man is really mortal. Everything is so temporary. Today, we could be in good health thinking we are invincible and that nothing can touch us; and in the blink of an eye we could be gone. We are just dust that the Lord breathed the breath of life into and made whole.

At this crossroad of my life, I felt I could not go on any longer. My wishes were that the Lord would just skip the next few days and transport me to the end. On this note, I was saddened, distraught, dismayed, and feeling sorry for myself. I cried out with a big shout and I reached out to my heavenly Father knowing I am a sinner who needs His help. I was physiologically tired and overwhelmed. I was physically wounded and suffering and spiritually needed God.

This was one of the moments when the seeds of my faith that were planted over forty years ago began to bear fruit. God became my Papa. I could hear Him whispering to me words of encouragement and support. The Bible verses came alive. These were the moments when I had no strength and had to rely upon the Word to guide me through these very dark days. My faith was never more real to me and Jesus' love was more evident than at those moments when my joy could not sustain me. I leaned on Him.

This was the time He said, "*my daughter Yvonne, again I heard your voice. You are almost there but it is not over until I, God, say so. I need to stencil and scrub you down a little bit more so you will have absolutely no doubt of whom I am.*"

Revelation 1:8 "*I am the Alpha and the Omega, the beginning and the end*" *says the Lord God,* "*who is, and who was, and who is to come the almighty God.*"

God was determined not to stop this make over process abruptly, just because I wanted it to end. It was the one time He was going to let me walk through the fire while holding my hand. This was the time he, God, was not bringing me to a halt in the middle of this procedure. I had to stay on this voyage where Jesus was the Captain, not Yvonne. I had to surrender completely and trust him thoroughly. "*Lord, I heard you clearly! I surrender my all to you! Please make a vessel out of me!*"

"*Show me what I need to do! I will trust!*" I have now come to realize how to smile in Christ and through pain! "*Please use me for whatever, where ever, I am ready!*" It could not be more evident that the Lord was talking to me.

Now, Yvonne, Matthew 11: 29 *"Take my yoke upon you and learn from me, for I am gentle and humble in heart, and you will find rest for your soul."*

The Lord let me know that He has a plan for my life, to go beyond where my mind couldn't comprehend at this moment. I have a message, a great task for you to do. I have my sheep out there for you to proclaim my glory. I have carved out a global task for you.

Ecclesiastes 9:11 says, *"I have observed something else under the sun. The fastest runner doesn't always win the race, and the strongest warrior doesn't always win the battle. The wise sometimes go hungry, and the skillful are not necessarily wealthy. And those who are educated don't always lead successful lives."*

It is all decided by chance, by being in the right place at the right time. Permit me to create you into the image of a warmer, more sensitive, wholehearted, gracious, patient and longsuffering person you need to be. I don't want you to be impatient and discouraged at the drop of one word.

The Lord wanted me to give up self completely and depend solely on him. If he had transported me across those days, I would have missed the magic of his wonders. I would not have had a convincing testimony to share of the awesomeness of God that I now love and cherish dearly. I know how to smile even though the pain penetrated every bit of my bone. So many times Satan tried to steal my smile away; but never have I been surer, I was going to liberate and unshackle myself from all the chains, doubt, worry, and self by seizing and recapturing my smile in this heartrending time of my life.

Oh, how I am learning to smile even through pain. Oh, how I am learning to smile when I can't see my way out. Nevertheless, I am going to rely on God still; because he is the ultimate wise God. With my papa Jesus, I can do all things through the strength of Him! I came to the realization, I was not 21 years old, that naive, foolish, inexperienced, clueless childlike person, and I am a mature Christian Woman. I had to live an exemplary life; one that would draw men to Christ.

One day one of my 'mothers' came to see me. As I heard the doorbell ring, I slowly, headed toward the door by muscling up every ounce of strength I could find with this big colorful shirt hanging off my blistered, raw, reddened, and irritated skin. Upon opening the door, my mother was confronted with my inflamed breast area. Not expecting to see me in so much pain she said, "I don't have to ask how you are, I can see it my love." That was when she shouted to the Lord asking him, *"How much can my daughter take?"* She then spun right around and went to her car.

I headed back upstairs, went to the window and could see her sitting in her car looking as if she was praying.

Days after, she told me just before she rang the doorbell she spoke with my husband and he was asking "how much more can one person take?" but she didn't realize how bad the situation was until she saw it. She said she could not get the image out of her mind so she diligently prayed for healing.

I got through it with the encouragement of my husband telling me to "hold on". My Facebook friends were sending me quotes to say I inspired them and that I could make it. My children said that the Lord would be my stronghold at this crossroad of my life. *"Oh my God, even though I felt as if you were not there, I will still trust!"* This was when I established in my mind that I would and must start a ministry. The goal of the ministry would be to let everyone know about my Papa, who brought me out of my darkest moments and to help educate women about this dreadful disease. I wished for no-one else to travel this journey!

My cancer journey was designed for me and only me. This shoe was made for Yvonne Headley Dunkley to wear on this excursion which was paved with doctors, medical machines, mothers from Lithonia SDA Church , Facebook friends, my children, my dear husband, Auntie Bev, and many more friends and family. I had to walk the street called Breast Cancer, with the big red signs of calcification and the landmarks of mastectomy. To the right nineteen lymph nodes were removed. To the left was a chest port for six rounds of chemotherapy. Straight ahead were thirty-five sessions of radiation. The bridge of ovarian surgery loomed and if you crossed over to the right-hand side a blood clot was waiting.

I could not bypass, deflect, or make a U-turn, because Jesus was waiting ahead with His arms wide open ready to lead the way. My God had given me the apparatus I needed for the race. He gave me enough of His blood for energy, equipped me with the Holy Spirit, armed me with His righteousness, and gave me enough power to soar like an eagle. He gave me the capacity to bear every inch of the pain. I needed to travel this life-threatening road so I would have no doubt of God's ability to carry me. So, I could proclaim His message strongly that every road we take, every trial we have; every crossroad we reach he will constantly abide strengthen, and carry us through our storms. All I had to do was depend on Him. In Him my strength would be renewed every morning.

When I took my eyes off Him for a second to look at the burned neck and missing breast, I immediately told the doctors and myself, "I can't go any further." I felt self-pity instead of calling on my Savior; but I could still hear my Savior saying,

Isaiah 41:10 says, *"Yvonne fear not, for I am with you; be not dismayed, for I am your God; I will strengthen you, I will help you, I will uphold you with my righteous right hand"*. "Hallelujah!"

I thank you Lord for your help even though I did not deserve it. Thank you for being there when my heart was filled with so much anguish and I felt all alone.

This was a time when I saw God's special love for me. How He blessed me. I now recognize that I am of a royal priesthood. I was comforted and confident that He was walking with me through the valley of the shadow of death, and all I had to do was to lay all my cares on Him, because He cared for me. The Lord knows how to get our attention, and Lord do I know how far you will go just to have me with you in the earth made new!

I did not pick my fight, my fight came to me and I had to choose which road to take. And thank God, my past groomed me for this fight. *"Thank you Jesus, you are awesome. You are worthy to be praised. There is none like you!"*

With the encouragement of my family, Facebook friends, support group, and, above all, God, I was able to graduate from radiation therapy with my thirty-five sessions. Well done! *"Thank you God, I made it one more time. You stood by my side. You loved me so much that you followed me into the shadow of death all the way."*

After my last thirty-five sessions of radiation with all that I went through, I felt I needed some tender loving

care. I could get that only in my home land, Jamaica. For me, Jamaica is where the transparent waters have healing power and the sand is crystal clear. The beaches are clean and the air is full of the smell of jerk chicken grilling on the wood stove and fried escovitched red snapper, with yellow onions and scotch bonnet peppers, with the vinegar dripping from the fish and festival. Not to mention the big, yellow East Indian mango, sweet sop, golden apple and roasted breadfruit with ackee and salt fish. It is a place of serenity and tranquility. Oh to be awakened by the chirping of the birds and crowing of the cocks and fowls!

With the help of my sister Angella Headley and my friend Pauline, I boarded a Delta airline flight in a big shirt that hung from my raw, red, burned skin. On approaching the island, I was excited to see the blue Caribbean water that awaited me. I spent a week with Angela's mother just going to the beach and trying to find solace in God. Then uncle Bousie drove me from Montego Bay to Portmore where my Auntie Cherry had arranged for someone to care for me. I was given baths, fed in my bed, and my pillow was repeatedly fluffed by my dear aunt. After a week of real loving treatment, I felt much better. They took me to Port Royal where we ate steamed fish and bammy and drank coconut water by the roadside. A day or two my wonderful husband surprised me in Jamaica and we had a blast. I just totally forgot I was weak and made the best of the situation. I was truly taken care of by all the people I came across. I had a wonderful time with everyone.

For me, my past experience taught me that in everything, good or bad, I must give God the glory and share it with others. In 2010, I was undergoing chemotherapy which left me physically challenged. By September 22, 2012, two years later, I had started a book, a mission, and a ministry for Breast Cancer Awareness. How did that happen? I have allowed my healer to fix me up enough so that I am able to share the good news of how Jesus Christ carried me from the shadow of death.

CHAPTER 3

A Disillusioned Bride

Reflections on my Past

Someone asked me why I think it is necessary to document my journey through life. From the core of my heart, I believe that my experience is not unique. At this very moment, there are people going through the same pain or similar situations, and others will go through it in the future. If I can help someone, yes, even one soul, from being torn apart, one heart from bleeding just like how mine did. If I can help one child to know that rejection hurts, but the soul can find healing in the blood of Christ. If I can help others as I travel along then my life shall not be in vain. I am not here to change the whole world. I will focus on sowing one tiny seed that can convert one soul, then another and another. Yes, my life on earth will be worth living.

I believe whenever I laugh, I take the chance of looking crazy. I believe whenever I reach out to a stranger, I take the chance of being rejected. I am thankful to God for allowing me to take the chance in loving my husband. Refusing to, I would have lost my jewel that was sent from God to me. The man that sits on the sideline and wishes for something may never get it. I chose to write this book and share my life story. My story of how my early years' growing up has set the precedent in my adulthood. How my adulthood shaped the rest of my life of who I chose to be for the rest of my life. I will take the risk in disclosing my life story about being a struggling young mother. I am taking the risk to free myself from my past and I hope it will inspire and help others. I believe we are conduits sent from God to help others.

I want to tell and show the world how not having that connection with God can make a difference in your life. Twenty years ago, I had to travel this same road and fell in the same potholes in order for God to get me where I am today in life. My Father had to allow Satan to tear me apart so he could rebuild me and have me prepared for His ministry. He had to toughen me up for today; my present.

I now believe that God has a task for each one of us on earth. God had a job for Jonah but he talked himself out of the task. God had to take him down another road where he found himself in the dark belly of a great fish. God had a job for Saul. God met him on the road to Damascus and blinded him so that he could see his true calling. Gifts and tasks from God are like a puzzle. When everyone does their part, the puzzle comes together perfectly. God knows our limits more than we ourselves do, because He is God. He created us. Sometimes the answers are staring us in the face, but we choose to ignore them. We sit comfortably and look back hoping things will fit together, when all this time we are sitting on a part of the puzzle. It is easy to have a Jonah syndrome. Well, God had a job for Jonah and David could not do it, because God had one for David too. Each one of us has a unique purpose.

The journey of life may not take me where I want to go, but my experiences are matchless. When the road is filled with stones and cracks, if I focus on my Savior and remember to look to Christ and then leap out in faith, only then will my dreams bear fruits. Only when I touch the hem of His garment will I find my true purposefulness in life.

My trials have borne ministries for children and for breast cancer awareness. These ministries are to help children and women to create and to have the experience of healthy self-image, self-esteem, and self-worth.

As I reflect on my previous experiences, I can truly say that my trials have helped me to overcome some of the feelings that I fought with over the years when I did not know what God was preparing me for. Although it is very difficult to relate to or identify with the mixed feelings I harbored over the years, I thank God for bringing healing to my soul and for the people with whom I have shared my life and family. From this vantage point, I can look back at some of my darkest moments and claim victory over the devil and his angels.

For many years, I have carried the pain of not understanding why I felt animosity between my family and our extended family. Little did I know back then that each of us had our own struggles and burdens that made it harder for us to help each other through the storm.

Today, I claim victory over these experiences. Today I proclaim my declaration of my past pain and with the most sincere and honest respect and admiration for my husband and his family. I share my past knowing that my yesterday was yesterday. I am embracing today's jubilation and a family that I love with all my heart. Walk with me through this wilderness, through my life's journey of searching for my way in the valley of the shadow of death where, as a young mother and wife at the age of twenty-two, my mind and body were fighting against all odds to protect my love, my children, and our future.

Take a Walk with me Down Memory Lane

I am a special and extraordinary child. There is none like me in the past, today, or in the world to come. My mom had me when she was forty-five and in comparison to my peers, it appeared as if I grew up with my grandmother. Growing up, my sphere of influence was an Adventist Christian home, school, and church, with all three being one and the same. I was not streetwise. Many things that I learned were taught to me by my peers. I saw the world as black and white, good or evil. To quote a Jamaican, "I was really a wash-belly baby meaning the last child a woman gives birth to." My mother thought she was going through menopause or had a tumor, when in fact she was pregnant with me. I grew up with the children of my older siblings—my nephews and nieces, as playmates.

I lived an extremely sheltered life. For example, I was not allowed to go downtown on Christmas Eve, the major shopping night of the holidays. The event was called Grand Market, but because it was not considered "Christian enough," I could not go with my friends.

I graduated from Harrison Memorial High School in Montego Bay, Jamaica in 1982, and then moved on to West Indies College, now Northern Caribbean University (School of the Prophets). While I was at West Indies College, I met my first husband. He was handsome, very intelligent, kind, and family-oriented. He had beautiful brown eyes that I thought I could see the world through. He graduated a year before I did and went to my High School to teach accounting. Since he did not know anyone in Montego Bay, my mother took him in like a son.

A year later, in 1984, I graduated from college. We got married March 31, 1985. We had a home in Catherine Hall in Montego Bay where we lived happily. He was teaching high school and I was the accountant at a local electrical company. We were classified as middle class. I had a great relationship with his family and he had a great one with mine too. After a year and a half of trying we could not get pregnant. We sought profession-al help and we were told that his sperm count was OK. Without being given any diagnosis of my own fertility, I assumed that I was the one who was preventing our getting pregnant. I left the doctor's office feeling useless and ashamed.

Months afterward, my mother-in-law came to visit with us. Apparently, my husband should have broken some bad news to me and had neglected to do so. My mother-in-law, as a good mother should be, was not comfortable sitting at the dinner table and eating the food I had lovingly prepared, knowing the terrible thing her son had done. When she could not keep her silence any longer, she addressed both her son and me. She revealed to me that her son had gotten another woman pregnant in Kingston, their hometown.

I was devastated, angry, and ashamed. I felt guilt and embarrassment because I could not get pregnant. At the young age of twenty-one, I did not know what to do in that type of a situation. So the next morning I awoke af-ter a turbulent and restless night and went to my mother and asked if she knew anyone in America. She told me she had a niece there and that was all I wanted to hear. I felt like such a failure that I didn't even confide in my mom what the situation was about.

The next day I went to the United States embassy, where I obtained a visa and fled the country. I did not want to deal with issues that I had no control over.

There is much to say about my mother-in-law. My mother-in-law embodied the term "Christian." She was a mother not only to her own children, but to all. She embraced people the way God wanted it. My relation-ship with her was one of love and mutual respect. As a matter of fact, I learned later that once her son's baby was born, she took the baby and raised him as her own.

That was the kind, endearing person my mother-in-law was. May her soul rest in peace!

After receiving my American visa, I came to the land of opportunity for a new beginning. I came through JFK airport, where I took a taxi to Crown Heights, Brooklyn, New York. Upon arriving at my destination, I was in a state of disbelief. One could call it culture shock. The taxi driver stopped at my destination and I asked if he was sure I was at President Street. He said, "Lady, what is your address again?" I told him the address again. And he said, "This is President Street between Schenectady and Troy." The area I found myself in reminded me of the worst part of Jamaica and here I was supposedly, in the land of plenty where the streets were supposed to be paved with gold. I was in a state of shock, looking at this grey-washed, graphite-looking, four-story building. I paid the cab driver and with my suitcase in hand began my new life!

As I approached the graffiti covered building, you could see the loud young guys hanging out on the step welcoming me to America. I timidly walked toward the door of the apartment. I tried to build courage as I passed the young guys. As I opened the door of the building, I could see the supermarket flyers and other papers colorfully scattered all over the floor of the hallway. I hurriedly walked up the stairway to the second floor where I knocked at the door. My cousin opened the door and greeted me excitedly. As I entered in through the narrow passage, I could see the living area straight ahead. She showed me her room and told me she had a roommate who lived in the other one. While she was talking to me, I wondered where I was going to sleep.

As the night approached, she told me that I would be sleeping in her girlfriend's room. This room had a single bed and a full-sized bed. While we were talking, the roommate's thirteen year old son came in and dropped down on his bed. In all there were four people in this two bedroom apartment already.

I lived with my cousin and her roommate for about seven months. Her roommate knew the owner of a jerk chicken restaurant and she found me a job there. It was there that I met Colin (my new husband) in October of 1986. I was initially not enamored with him, but with persistence and kindness he won my heart. He seemed to be kind, hardworking, and very humble. At that time I needed a friend. I was in a foreign land with few family members or friends.

Being the ambitious person I was, I got a studio apartment in Brooklyn within six months of my arrival in New York City. My salary was $120 per week, working sixty hours and six days a week. At that time I was very happy for the job, because my mother was retired and since she had always worked for herself, she did not have a pension. She was also raising my sister's children. I was able to send money to my mother and to pay my rent and day-to-day expenses. Thank God for my mother as an example.

When I got the apartment, I had to pay one month's rent, one month's deposit, and the realtor's fee. That day, I moved into my fourteen-by-fourteen studio apartment with zero dollars left. I happily slept on the floor until the following week when I could afford to buy a bed. I had my own keys and it was my castle and I gave God thanks for it.

Colin and I joined hands and hearts on September 31, 1987 at City Hall in Manhattan, New York. We were penniless and with just my sister-in law, Angela as our witness, we embarked on our new life ahead. Not knowing much about each other's backgrounds, Colin and I started a journey into the unknown.

Struggle Ahead

Colin and I were elated. He had a job at a Bank in Manhattan, where he worked nights in the Computer room. I had breakfast waiting for him when he came home every morning. As we started our family, we realized that life was no longer just about us. It was about caring, nurturing, and preparing precious souls for the kingdom. The blessing of having children was a wonderful thing, but then we realized that starting a family in our adopted homeland with no family support was not an easy task.

Chadeesia's Birth

When I had my first bout of nausea, I thought I had a serious bug. When it continued for the next three days, my husband told me that I was pregnant. I thought he was joking or simply wrong, because I knew I could not get pregnant. He encouraged me to see a doctor. When the doctor confirmed it, I felt as if I had a "vertical shift." Heaven had literally opened up for me.

My husband and I were very happy about our pregnancy. We had fun watching my "bump" grow. Having this baby was the delight of our life and we were like two peas in a pod. We had lots of laughter and joy. We were two happy people walking on air. He accompanied me to every doctor's appointment. I felt I had found peace with myself at the age of twenty-two.

On July 31, 1988, my husband took me in to have our baby at Brookdale Hospital in Brooklyn. After delivering Chadeesia, the doctor realized she had jaundice, so Chadeesia was left in the hospital for three days. Upon leaving the hospital with me, my husband was told by the nurse to get a breast pump for me, because I would need it over the course of breastfeeding. After I was discharged from the hospital, he took me home. As he inserted the key in the door, our phone inside the house was ringing. After he answered the phone, he proceeded to make me comfortable by fluffing the pillow, giving me my pills, and setting a glass of water beside me; then he said, "I will be back soon." I thought he was going to get the breast pump.

I waited for Colin to come back but more than two hours went by. I waited a little bit longer until 4:30 pm. By then, it had been over four hours. I got nervous wondering what had happened to him. I called his mother's home and she answered the phone. I greeted her and asked if she had seen my husband. She proceeded to ask me what I wanted with Colin. I told her that I had my baby and had just come home from the hospital. I explained that Chadeesia was left in the hospital and that my husband had left many hours ago and that I was concerned about him. She replied, "He took his sisters and their children to the amusement park at Coney Island." I exclaimed, "What!" I was profoundly shocked. Her reply to me was, "That's the way I brought them up, to look after one another. They must stick to each other."

I could not make any sense of what she said to me. I hung up the phone. I could not believe what I had just heard. I was amazed and flabbergasted. Surely she would wish the best for another person, especially her own flesh and blood. That day while I was lying in bed feeling so melancholy, my mother called me from Jamaica. She said that she had had a dream about me and wanted to know if I was okay. I told her what had just transpired between Colin's mother and me. Her response to me was, "Don't worry my dear; the Lord will take you through." We both cried, and then she called Angela, my brother's wife, who was living a bit far from me and asked her to take care of me.

When my husband came home I was so angry. The first thing I asked him was whether his sisters knew I had had the baby. His reply was "Yes, I told them." That made me even angrier, because each of them had a child, so they should have known what childbirth was like and that I needed help and support. For them to have told him to take them to an amusement park while I sat waiting on a breast pump was beyond my comprehension. I told my husband, "I don't know where you people come from, but in my world a man takes care of his wife, children, and his home and the extended family supports."

This was my first true introduction to their family dynamic. After that there were numerous incidents similar to the one previously mentioned and they happened quite frequently. Without going into details, I want to just remind you, my readers, that there are no escaping trials, problems, and stress.

Stress is a part of our lives! How we handle stress can have a negative impact on our health or allow us to live in grace happily with God. I was just twenty-two years old in a new country and not having experience and the strength to cope added to the stress and made the situation more toxic.

Each one of our trials comes in different packages. Each one of us has to bear our own cross. My ordeal will be different from yours, but the key thing to remember is that we have a God who specializes in our welfare and care. God said,

John 14:27 *"Peace I leave with you, my peace I give unto you; not as the world gives, give I unto you. Let not your heart be troubled, neither let it be afraid."*

If we take our cross and lay it at his feet, he will take care of our battles. If I had known then what I know now at the age of forty-six, just maybe the stress of life would not have caused my health to deteriorate or have slowly eaten me up and manifested itself in sickness. Although scientists have not come up with the true reason for the cause of cancer, there are lots of speculations or theories of causative factors. I personally believe that stress has 90% to do with illness. Stress breaks the body down.

Colin and I sought counseling from our pastor and I tried to empathize with what my husband was going through, being torn between his extended family and being loyal to his immediate family. Colin always wanted to "do the right thing" by standing by his family, but all we would hear was, "a mi one mine mi pinckney dem so send him home to me!" (Translation-"I took care of my children alone, so let me have my son back!").

During that time in my marriage, I felt like I was fighting against evil forces. My husband was riddled with the burden and guilt of what his father did not do and feeling responsible for his mother. My counselor would say, "Do not take it personally, because it does not matter who her son married, it would have been the same behavior." But I struggled with how to not take it personally when I felt as if all this hatred was directed at me. My mother-in-law did not even give herself a chance to know me.

The Birth of my Second Child

Coleen, my second child, just seemed to complicate my marriage and experience with the extended family even more. I felt as if having another child triggered something in her. By then, I began to feel like I wanted to get out of my marriage.

Now I was faced with marital issues, again. Although these were different I still had no control over them. I prayed, I cried, I complained, and I talked to my husband, but all I could hear was, "Things are going to get better."

Personally, I thought I had jumped from the frying pan with my first husband into the fire in my second marriage. I had absolutely no other issues with my husband, Colin. He had the kindest, humblest, and sweetest personality. My frame of reference about how a mother-in-law should operate was totally shattered. I truly believe that knowing God makes a world of a difference in every situation.

Everything I felt and understood appeared very conflicting.

1. My own mother's treatment toward her sons' wives was always respectful. It was a delight in the real sense of the word for my mother to love, embrace, and reach out to all her grandchildren.
2. My first mother-in-law had been like a second mother. Her actions toward me showed that she genuinely loved me.
3. The Bible said that I could not divorce my partner except for sexual immorality, and "*who marries a divorced woman commits adultery*" (Matthew 19:9). I felt as if I had no biblical grounds to leave.

I can recall my mother taking me to the hospital when I was seventeen years old to visit my brother's newborn child because my brother had migrated to the USA. My mother had been totally unaware of the situation beforehand. My caring mother took the initiative and we went to the hospital to see the young lady and the baby, which my mother wholeheartedly accepted without even talking to my brother. Now I was married living with my husband. I thought the same love that was exhibited from my mother to this lady in the hospital, should be expected from my new mother-in-law. However, that was where the comparison ended.

I was at a loss to understand some of my experiences, but my mother would say to me, "Polly (my nickname), pray without ceasing to God for his covering, protecting, shielding, and his mercy for your children. Exodus 20:5 says that *"the sin of the fathers shall visit the first, second, third, and fourth generations"*, for that I should make the Bible literally my guide.

The psychological stress of confronting my situation was beyond my coping resources. My inexperienced mind could not wrap itself around all this. It was mind-boggling and overwhelming. By then, I was twenty-four years old with an infant and a two-year-old, refusing to accept my husband's mother's philosophy for me to send back her son to her at the expense of abandoning his immediate family. Refusing to give up my husband, even though at times I just wanted to give up, I spent many years, wondering how someone could be that bitter and cold.

Accepting someone's beliefs does not mean they are right, but it means I should respect them, because that person believes in them. Respecting this family member's behavior, even though it made no sense to me, would have allowed me to move on from the denial stage.

And it would have worked only if I was living close to Christ. Living close to Christ helps us to allow Christ to deal with the stressor and to manage the situation or the battle. Thus, allowing one to move on.

I recognize now at that period in my life, I was not ready or prepared by my parents and teachers for the real world. The real world comes not just in black and white. Things are not just good or evil. Things come in varying shades of grey. The idea that a mother would want her son back and choose to support only her daughters and their children, with the exclusion of her son's was too much for me. As a sibling, I often wondered if I would take the stand by just looking on as a spectator and watch my mother behave in such an unseemingly manner. I believe even though the behavior of my mother may have continued, I would not allow my mother to believe my silence means consent, and thus, giving her the right to continue destroying my brothers' life. It is amazing how we can take no stand, but yet our silence is even stronger than if we had said something. This concept was very difficult for me to understand. I could not understand the whole matter. I was at a loss. I found myself in something that was bigger than me. I believe that whenever we as human beings can understand a part of the whole puzzle, it is easier to accept; but none of this even made sense.

All I ever wanted was to get married, love, laugh, and live happily ever after! What was wrong with that? Now it seemed to me that this was a fairy tale. Is it that this kind of life does not exist in the real world? Is it that I am too naive and idealistic? I believe we should treat people with respect and dignity, love, give, share, watch each other's back; embrace each other; and trust and live as if there is no tomorrow, just because God says so. Can't we reach out to each other without hesitation or a hidden motive and just love?

Having all the cards stacked against me, I decided to follow my husband's advice and believe things would get better. I felt that if I had known the kind of family I was getting into, I would not have married my husband, because life is too short to allow anyone to treat you callously and heartlessly. How could one live happily, knowing that you have nieces and nephews that you did not care about and did not even know, even though they lived ten to twenty minutes away? This was beyond me!

I wanted to leave this relationship so badly, but I knew it would not be in my best interest, because of the following reasons:

1. I loved my husband
2. My husband was filing my immigration papers.
3. I was in a foreign land with limited support.
4. I was the mother of two little children only two years old and five months old.
5. Most of all, this was my second marriage within four years and I was only twenty-four years old.

Colin continued to work at the bank in the computer department. It was a very good job that his cousin was instrumental in getting him. Meanwhile, I was doing a variety of odd jobs to help with the household expenses. Not yet having my green card and a work permit, I decided that come what may, I was going to succeed. Failure was not an option.

At one point, my friend, Delores got me a good-paying job in Brooklyn taking care of an elderly lady. After having my second child, Coleen, I gave my mother-in-law the job. In retrospect, I believe I gave her the job, because I wanted her to like me and to reduce her animosity towards me. Then again, my friends would say that I was always giving, trying to fix and begin anew. Over the years, I ensured she was always invited to birthday parties, school graduations, christenings, and all the other important events in the children's lives. I could probably count her attendance to these occasions.

After the births of our two older girls, my seventy-year-old parents back in Jamaica encouraged us to send the girls to them just until we laid a firm foundation. We sent our girls to Jamaica, which allowed us to re-group, work harder, and purchase a home on Long Island. We then brought our angels, Chadeesia and Coleen back to the United States.

CHAPTER 4

Through The Fire

Our girls came back from Jamaica to us. Our family was complete once again. I remember it was like an oasis, we were happy during this period. Colin and I were progressing and feeling happy within. Regardless of the entire negative external factors surrounding us; we vowed to make it come "high river with tidal waves"! I tried to dismiss my outside influences but Satan stood tall. With God's sense of humor, two years after the return of our children from Jamaica, we found ourselves pregnant again with our third child, Yvonna.

Because of all the issues we were having with my extended family, I thought I was not emotionally prepared to bring another child into this miserable and gloomy world, to expose another one of God's precious souls to such chaos. There are certain issues in life we don't want to face and go through the pain of dealing with again. I could not talk about my children and my mother-in-law in the same sentence. If I did, the pit of my stomach would hurt. I could not cope mentally, because in my mind I did not want to go back to that nasty unresolved problem. This issue was very real to me, so, in that frame of mind, I found myself at an abortion clinic, contemplating the unthinkable.

"Psychological abuse often contains strong emotionally manipulative content designed to force the victim to comply with the abuser's wishes. It may be emotional abuse in this sense when it is designed to cause emotional pain to victims or to 'mess with their heads' in attempts to gain compliance and counter any resistance. Alternatively, psychological abuse may occur when one victim is forced to watch another be abused in some fashion. Psychological abuse is often not recognized as abuse early on and can result in serious sequel (psychological after effects) later on" (Types of Abuse, by Kathryn Patricelli, MA. Updated Dec, 15, 2005).

Ephesians 6:12 "*We wrestle not against flesh and blood but against principalities in high places*".

Follow me into that wilderness I found myself into, at an intersection in my life, in an abortion clinic. What happens in an abortion clinic? Could someone just pinch me and let me know what happens there! I felt my husband's mother was emotionally brutal to my children and I and it had driven me to the point of no return. It is interesting how fear can enslave us and cause us to do things we would generally not have done had we been happy and emotionally independent.

Hence, I found myself in an abortion clinic; feeling confused, perplexed, bewildered, and disoriented, when ironically, years before I thought I was unable to get pregnant and had desperately wanted a child. "Now look where I was", I thought to myself.

We are an ungrateful people. It seems God cannot do enough to please us. In the summer we say we are too hot. He gives us winter and then we say it is too cold. One minute we want rain, the next minute we want drought. I am so happy God is not like man. He is extremely accommodating and longsuffering!

As I sat in the chair, waiting to hear my name called by the nurse at the abortion clinic, there was a conflict going on inside my head. All the reasons I should abort the baby came up before me. My main reason was I did not want to bring another child into the world to face the rejection of Colin's mother; and I felt justified. The waves of desperation were drowning me and I felt like God forgot me. I felt all alone, with no escape. Just a few years ago, I had to send my two children to my mother who was in her seventies. It would not be fair to her to ask for help again. I was also thinking about my husband. If anything happened to me in the clinic, my husband would not know where I was.

Nevertheless, that small voice that I heard faintly said, "*My daughter, I heard your cry. I am right here carrying you. I don't want you to worry about anything, I have everything under control. You are covered by the blood that I, Jesus, shed on Calvary's cross. Yvonne, I specifically died for you, because I knew before you knew that this day was coming. I have big things in the future for you to do and that is why I will not deliver you now. But you have to go through these trials and tribulations alone. I, God, made provision for you. Allow me to lift you up with the right hand of my righteousness. Let me take you out of here*".

"*It is I who gives life and it is I who can take it. I create and I destroy. Leave vengeance to me; allow me to take you home in the arms of your two beautiful daughters and your loving husband. Come, come my beloved, to your husband and two angels. I will set you free one day, but for now, you have not reached the mark. You are not ripe in my gospel as yet. I want to use you so you can travel the four corners of the world and share my message of how good I am. You are not fit to be delivered, but remember, it is I who determines when you are ready and ripe to be harvested…You have a huge task to do for me.*"

"*Hallelujah, Hallelujah, Hallelujah, Hallelujah. All praises to you, God. You are Holy, Amen*", I shouted in my mind.

Suddenly, I heard my name being called, "Yvonne Dunkley," and the nurse with my chart in her hand was saying, "Follow me." Did you hear what she said to me, "Follow me"? How many of us are following the voice of Satan. Feeling flushed, faint, and confused, I used my right hand to push my weak body up from the chair and somehow I found myself in my car in the parking lot crying. The Lord carried me away from that place.

My God said, "*Despite all these things, the overwhelming victory is mine, but only through Christ, who loved me*".

Romans 8:38 says, "*Nothing can ever separate us from God's love. Neither death nor life, neither angels nor demons, neither our fears for today nor our worries about tomorrow, not even the powers of hell can separate me from God's love. No power in the sky above or in the earth below. Indeed, nothing in all creation will ever be able to separate me from the love of God that is revealed in Christ Jesus our Lord*". Glory to the new born king, only you alone are worthy to be worshipped!

What I have come to know now, I wish I knew then. I would not have mentally agonized and grieved that way. I cannot change my yesterday, but I can change my today and look for a brighter tomorrow. Yes, I can accept my cross and make a difference in my life and in others. I am determined that my life must be a beacon today, because I must see my Jesus. I now empty myself from the baggage of the world; forgive my extended family and anyone else I have ever held a grudge against. I pray they will forgive me too. In order to be saved I must forgive. I believe forgiveness is good for the person who wrongs you, but more so for your own soul. I no longer see myself as a victim, but as an overcomer. Not even the wizards of the underworld will isolate or snatch me again from my Father. My God's grace is sufficient for me.

As a matter of fact, I don't want to change my past, because as a result of my grief in the past, I am more sensitive to the needs of children. Whenever I hear of a person diagnosed with breast cancer, my entire being responds in compassion. So the only way I can do my part is to bring awareness to everyone. I want to help. "*Use me Lord. Use me*", is my plea.

At thirty years old, I was feeling misplaced, thinking the struggle with my husband's family was too much for me. I want you to know that it is not over until God says so. I had to walk this road. If you ever find yourself in an abortion clinic, then you should run. Are you hearing me—run, as though you hear that terrorists were coming for you! Do you remember the story of Joseph? God had a plan for him. He had to walk the same road that led his siblings to sell him; the same path to Potiphar's house. Why? God had a plan for him.

I believe I can use the analogy of Joseph in the Bible with all the trials that I went through in my twenties. God allowed it, because in His ultimate wisdom He had a bigger plan for me. I believe God wants us to use everything we go through in life as a blessing for others. I had to go through fire like gold does in order to come out dross-free twenty years later. Having gone through mental and physical trials, I am now truly prepared to be used by God in the awesome task of Breast Cancer Awareness.

My God had a plan for me. The only way I could learn what it was, was for me to get personally close to Jesus. I needed to build a rapport with Him and trust Him as if my life depended on it. My God knew long before I did that I would have breast cancer and He wanted to entrust this ministry to me. I always tell my children that the more you study for the examination, the easier it will be. The purpose of my past was to prepare me for today. And on these grounds, I can only love everyone, in spite of and despite their behaviors. I learned late in life that Satan was just distracting me, because he must have had a clue about the awesome future God had in store for me and wanted to derail me and ruin God's mighty plan for my life. *"In the name of the mighty Jesus, Satan you are a liar and a swindler!"*

Through Colin's Eyes

I left the abortion clinic with the intention of having my baby with the help of God. I had Yvonna, my third child, with the guiding hands of the Lord. Within three months of my pregnancy, I started to feel pain in my right leg whenever I stood or walked. I had to leave my job, because Yvonna was lying on my sciatic nerve, which made me immobile. My mother came from Jamaica to help me with my family. After six months, she had to return to Jamaica, because she was only allowed six months in the United States. She left and my heart pained, because her help meant so much to us especially at this point in my life.

When I went to the hospital to have the baby, I had major complications. The doctors did not realize that the baby weighed over ten pounds, because I was eating my troubles away, literally. They insisted that I have the child the natural way. Have you ever heard of the song, *"One set of footprints in the sand"* by **Mary Stevenson?** Well, God carried me through this. The doctors had me on my knees with the palms of my hands on the bed, pushing. The doctor said, "Gravity will pull the child out." Well gravity failed! She then put me on my back and gave me oxygen through my nose. It was one of the most uncomfortable positions I have ever found myself in.

I was very frustrated and miserable, because the pain was so severe. The pain was like nothing I had ever experienced before. She proceeded to give me an epidural, which reduced the pain for a few minutes, and then it came back with a vengeance. I started to shout out through the pain. I felt as if I was speaking Jamaican patois, because the nurses and doctors could not understand me. But they knew whatever the language was it meant "take this child from me".

After eight hours of unbearable pain they took me to have a Caesarian section. When I was coming out of the anesthesia, I heard a voice saying, "Mrs. Dunkley, your tubes are not tied. Mrs. Dunkley, your tubes are not tied." I fought my way to have this child and all I asked the doctors to do was to tie my tubes. I signed the affidavit requesting them to do a tubal ligation.

The doctor did not do it because she thought I would want more children. I believed that this "thing," whatever it was, was not going to end. I felt like I just wanted to go back to sleep permanently. Have you ever felt like this, perhaps, when the world seems like it is too much? I was mentally upset, physically wounded, and spiritually confused.

When I finally came out of the anesthesia, I asked for my baby. The nurse said that the baby had to be flown to the Long Island Jewish Children's Hospital. I had been in labor for so long, the baby was in distress and her APGAR scores came back low. My husband went with the ambulance crew. Yvonna was born on November 24, 1994, on a Thanksgiving morning. I heard that when she reached the hospital, it was announced over the PA system that the turkey had arrived. There were other babies there, but Yvonna was over ten pounds, and arguably the biggest baby on the pediatric ward.

I was released from the hospital after two days, while Yvonna was still in the other hospital. Without the ability to understand my mental state, I felt like I needed my mother. Yes, my mother. Now, I know this was true postpartum depression. Thank the Lord my church sisters,

Mrs. Bramwell, Mrs. McInnis, Auntie Lyn, and many more of them were there for me.

Yvonna came home and I just felt more emotionally drained. I went to the doctor for my scheduled six-week checkup, only to find that I had a hernia. The doctors decided that I needed to have surgery to repair the hernia and do the tubal ligation at the same time. This was my second major surgery within six weeks. Then one night Yvonna could not breathe.

I called 911 to let them know the baby was not breathing properly, but I was so calm that the operator asked me to put the phone to the baby's chest. The quick thinking of that person saved my child's life that night. She was diagnosed with asthma. I can say thank God about this, because that was the only time she had an asthma attack.

After surgery on my hernia, I went in for my checkup only to find that the hernia had broken again. The doctor suggested that I do another surgery to cut into the old incision, now above my navel, which was to put a mesh as a cushion in my abdomen. It would fix the previous wound but extend it way above my navel. I felt very sad, dispirited, and stressed. This was my third major surgery within five months of giving birth!

I knew my husband was hurting but I felt listless. Colin was working two jobs while all this was happening. He would drive from Brentwood, Long Island to Rockland County (two hours both ways). On his way home he would stop at Newsday Co. (second job), then return home to look after Yvonna. "Oh how I love him!" As soon as Colin reached home, he would wash the baby bottles, wash all the clothes, and get Chadeesia and Coleen ready for school. "*Thank you Jesus, for such a dedicated and caring husband*". During this period I saw the core of my man and I truly grew to love him even more. God was also preparing him for today.

While I was slowly recovering from the various surgeries, my church sisters from Central Islip SDA Church rallied around us. Still, it seemed as if I could not emerge from the depression. I was wondering where was God. I needed Him to show up in my life, but I could not feel Him; or so I thought at that time. My mother was calling almost every day from Jamaica (which was very costly in those days). I remember one particular day just as if it was today. My mother called and I was crying and wishing she was there. She said to me, "I am praying for you, my dear." She had recognized that my laughter was gone and that I was going through too much. She told Colin to send the children home to her. Even though my mother was in her late seventies and retired, she took on the responsibility of caring for all three of my children, with the youngest only five months old. Her intention was for my husband to seek help for me. Colin then reached out to Auntie Cherry and Uncle Buddy, and my brother Paul and his wife, my "sister", Angela, in Maryland.

I would like to let everyone know that in the midst of every storm God has already arranged the right people for you. Don't feel sorry for yourself, but in prayer and supplications go down on your knees and ask Jesus to spin your wheels. "Thank you Jesus!" I could have lost my mind nevertheless Jesus kept me! I could have gone insane but Jesus kept me! I was bewildered, but Jesus covered me with his blood! He not only kept me, he is using me for greater things. "Thank you Jesus!" Society says that everything has to be going well for you to be happy. God says, it is when you are broken I can use you best, because then no one can say it was in their own strength.

"What a mighty God we serve!"

Psalm 23 says that He will walk with us *"through the valley of the shadow of death." He will cover us with his right hand of righteousness."*

2 Chronicles 20:9 *"If calamity comes upon us, whether the sword of judgment, or plague or famine, we will stand in your presence before this temple that bears your Name and will cry out to you in our distress, and you will hear us and save us."* That is how much he loves us.

Colin drove me to Maryland to stay with my brother Paul and Angela, but they had plans to go to Jamaica that same week. Satan knows just how to intervene; but Jesus had Auntie Cherry and Uncle Buddy right there for me. Considering my history with Colin's family, I was a little hesitant staying with them, but Colin said she was a very nurturing lady. They were the right people and I had to trust him. God knows just what you need at the right time. I stayed with my Auntie Cherry for a month and for the last week I was with Angela Headley. It was just what I needed in order to recuperate fully. Ann Marie, Aunt Cherry's daughter had just migrated to the USA. We all had a great time. We cooked and baked almost every day.. What I remember most about Auntie Cherry is that every morning after Uncle Buddy would leave for work, Auntie Cherry would call me and I would lay right under her arm beside her in bed. Just what the doctor ordered.
"Praises to all the mothers out there who can nurture and care for someone else's child as if for their own."

"Postpartum depression is real. It is a moderate to severe depression in a woman after she has given birth. It may occur soon after delivery, and up to a year. It is usually caused by changes in hormone levels and by non-hormonal factors. ~A.D.M. MEDICAL ENCYCLOPEDIA; last reviewed: September 19, 2012

Because of all the external factors and not wanting another baby to be exposed to all these issues, I was in the perfect mental state to experience postpartum depression at its worst. I stayed in Maryland long enough to recuperate and my "laughter" returned.

I believe a true sibling, neighbor, or family member will risk his position, his prestige and even his life for the welfare of another. After our children had returned home from Jamaica to live with us, we decided to file for Tanya, Colin's first child. I must point out here that *"God does not make mistakes."* The day we received the immigration papers and affidavits, I panicked because of all the negative stories about step-daughters and all the trials with outsiders that surrounded us. I went to my church elder, Pauline McInnis and talked with her about the situation. She got me on my knees and prayed with me. When we got up off our knees, she said to me, *"The Lord could not have sent her to a better home."* I then left with a joyous spirit, gathered all the necessary documents, and in a few months our blessed daughter became a part of the Dunkley household.

Even though Satan tried to enter my home many times, he could not prevail, because of all the prayers that were upon my family. I had my mother, my church sisters, Colin, and I with bleeding hearts, praying for God's presence to continue abiding in our home. I would like to touch on another subject right here. In this period of my life, I found my husband and I were praying some intense prayers. We would clinch our hands together, fall on our knees by our bedside and we would pray, because we realized we wanted our relationship to work and we could only make it through the grace of God.

Whenever we found ourselves in trouble, it is amazing how often we would pray and the intensity of the prayer. Think on these words!

However, as time passed, I was faced with challenges that I would not wish on anyone. One day, I heard Chadeesia, my eight-year old, shouting at her big sister Tanya, who was then fourteen years old. So I sat her down and asked her what was going on. She told me that her Grandma did not like her. I asked her where she had gotten this idea. She said that whenever Grandma called on the phone and she answered, Grandma would say, "Let me talk to Tanya." She would not even engage Chadeesia with even the simplest pleasantries. I sat Coleen who was six, Chadeesia who was eight and Tanya who was fourteen years old down to discuss this painful madness that even I as an adult could not understand. These are the moments I saw Satan for who he truly is, by working through the hearts of man. These are the times when I understand more when the bible says, Jeremiah 17:9

"The heart is deceitful above all things, and desperately sick; who can understand it?"

My heart burns and started to feel heavy; my hands and feet shivered and started to feel weak and my mind was blown away. If I never needed Jesus before in my life, I surely needed him right now, this instant!

Those were the times when I truly needed the heavenly Father for His wisdom. You see a few years ago, I tuned this lady out completely after all her temper tantrums, but when Tanya came to live with us she saw a new avenue to saddle me down. Did you know depending on how we deal with our stress, God can open up opportunities for us? I used this distasteful occasion to reinforce the need for my children to love each other. I used this chance to emphasize that even though the world says, she is your step-sister, she is really your sister. I unflinchingly, established in my children's mind that even though Tanya had another mother, she is my daughter too. Chadeesia wanted to know why Tanya was favored by grandma. In times like this, what do you tell an eight-year old who is feeling rejected by someone who should have been the love of her life? I found myself in a storm, in a never ending abyss. I had gotten myself engulfed in a marriage with one of the sweetest men God put on this earth, but he comes with a kind of baggage that hurt so badly one that he had totally no control over and now this baggage not only became my cross, but the children's too. It did not matter what he said or did, his mother had the last talk and action. Oh God! Oh how my heart engulfed with such sickening pain. Oh how I had it! Oh how the bottom of my belly longs to be quenched and my soul thirsts to be soothed from this torture. Oh how I had to go through the valley.

Lord, you did not deliver me from my pain, nevertheless I thank you for keeping me when I almost let go. I reached a point in my life where I could not understand what and why I was going through all this but through it all Lord, thank you for your grace and mercy that kept me sane. I, straightforwardly, let my children know they should continue to love each other. The love of Christ was evident in my children's lives as I have never seen this behavior in their life again, even though Satan tried numerous times again. For this Lord, I give you the praise!

This kind of behavior was directed at me over the years, but I did not know it was directed at my children, so bluntly too. At the time, I felt this was the ultimate level of unhealthy behavior that any child could be exposed to. I did not probe too much on my outside influence, because my mind was consumed with my children's psychological well-being and how I wanted my life to go. These were some of the unhealthy behaviors I experienced that allowed me to establish in my mind to reach out to children. I was faced with this situation and even though I did not have control over others' behavior toward me; I chose to make a difference in my life and in the lives of any and every child I come in contact with. This was the situation that made me want to write a book. Oh how I struggled and pondered on how on God's heavenly green planet, I could sit back, avert my eyes, mentally block it out and allow this unhealthy behavior to go on and not reach out to my brothers and their children. How could I be content within not wanting it for my children and look on it happening to others?

We as a society always wonder why "those children" grow up to be so angry. It is because "those children" grew up in resentment and an aggressive atmosphere and we shut our eyes while "those children" had to survive under such intense situations. Oh how we sit and say "those children" are not mine so I can wink my eyes and pass them. This selfishness is absolutely wrong!

Whenever our children live with hugs, kisses, laughter and warmth; they will learn to give, to smile, to be positive, and to be secure within.

Whenever our children grow up with patience around them; they will learn persistence and perseverance.

Whenever our children grow up with support around them; they will be successful in their endeavors and know how not to give in or give up.

When we undermine and allow our children to feel inferior, they will have absolutely no self-assurance, no self-reliance, and no self-esteem; thus society will be at a loss in the long run. Please remember this kind of behavior can happen quietly and have an indelible effect on children.

We often wonder why our children grow up to be so angry; it is because they grew up in a resentful atmosphere. We often wonder why our children cannot feel confident within; it is because they grew up being ridiculed day after day. We often wonder why our children grow up to be heartless; it is because they grew up in a hostile and unloving environment. We often wonder why our jails are full with our black boys; it is because they grew up without being encouraged or inspired and had no positivity around them. Life is absolutely too short for one to be so unkind and callous.

"There is no such thing as other people's children. They are all our children" ~Hillary Clinton

I believe whenever children have confidence in themselves, the victory is already won. Whenever that child steps out in life, even if he/she fails, that child will have the will power to brush off the dust from his/her shoe, get up and continue. Whenever a child harmonizes and synchronizes that willpower with God's promises, what a powerful child he/she becomes. That child will have a sense of wanting to accomplish his/her goal. That child will be able to move mountains. That child will be the next president of a great nation. That child will have the capability to see beyond his/her challenges. That child

will create solutions for today's and tomorrow's problems and achieve great things in this troublesome world.

I felt like Colin and I could do nothing to stop it, but we could certainly continue to stay on our knees with bleeding hearts and pray for God to protect us. After Tanya came to live with us, my church mothers and I prayed that Tanya's presence would be a blessing in our home and "Praise the Lord", it was.

Another accident that stands profoundly in my mine is, one evening after coming home from work, Tanya told me that Grandma wanted me to call her. I picked up the phone and I said hello and was greeted with shouting and cursing. I was told I must not let Tanya call me mother. Apparently, Colin's mother called my home and asked Tanya where I was. Tanya had told her Mommy was not home. She went ballistic, because Tanya called me mommy. She let me know in no uncertain words, "nuh let Tanya call yuh nuh madda!" (Translation: "Do not let my grandchild Tanya call you mother). I told her in a sweet way, that if she was acting like a good mother in-law then I would be calling her mother as well. I told her that I would pray for her.

She went on to say that she had asked Colin to let Tanya travel with her to Canada and that I was the one trying to prevent it. I told her that I had no clue what she was talking about. I also told her that Chadeesia perceives her action as not liking her by calling for Tanya and totally ignoring her and she needed to stop it. I told her she had four grandchildren in this house and that if she wanted to be in Tanya's life, she would have to accept all four of my children as they were a package deal! I refused to separate my children. Then she said, she did not want my three children. After she said that, I noticed the children were crying, because they heard their Grandma's bitter words. I realized then we were on speaker the whole time. I hung up the phone.

When I heard my mother-in-law utter the words, "I don't want your children," my emotions ran the gamut from disbelief to dismay, to disgust, and to a state of being appalled. I felt the burning in the pit of my stomach. It blew my mind!

I thought I needed Jesus then, but now I needed God; Jesus, the Holy Ghost and all the Angels in heaven. As I said before, I wish not to go into my other ninety five percent of pure torture, because my ordeal will be different from yours, but please remember there is a God who sits high and looks low. We sometimes think He is not hearing our cries and seeing our tears. I can testify that if anyone thinks there is no God above, I am here to let the world know my God is real. My Jesus has risen and has ascended to heaven. The Holy Spirit is still doing His job as a comforter. My family was given prickles in the saddle to carry on our backs, as if the saddle was not heavy enough. The edges of these prickles were as sharp as a two sided knife. For years I have washed it pierced into my husband's soul and drilled my heart leaving these gigantic holes. This thorn has grown so big that it was not just over powering my husband and me. Now, it is scorching the souls of my children and messing up the heads of my children. 'And we wonder why these children in society are so messed up?' From the bottom of my belly, the one that has pained me for over twenty years, I am here to let the world know my GOD carried us: my husband, my four children and I. In 2 Corinthians 12:7-10, Paul wrote about the thorn in his flesh, well this was mine. My family absolutely could not have bypassed this hell we found ourselves in. Oh how I wiped many tears from my blood shed eyes while writing this book. On that day, when I heard those words, what could I have done to help my family emotionally? Who could I call on that day when I heard the words, "I don't want Chadeesia, Coleen and Yvonna?" This was my cross and I had to carry it whether I liked it or not. You see, Jesus had a choice whether or not he wanted to carry our sins on His back. He knew in his infinite wisdom that the cross was going to be heavy, and even though he thought he knew it was heavy, Jesus is found in the Bible crying out to God for help. The Lord allowed me, Yvonne, to go through this terrible and heart wrenching time in my life. I was not asked or warned about anything on September 31, 1987. I dived in head first in my marriage. I came up fully soaked with tears dripping for many years to come. There were no short cuts, no detours, and certainly no dodging from those vile words, "mi nu want yu pickney them and a mi one mine mi pickney them." Through it all, I have learned to depend upon God!

Psalm 136:1-13 says, *"give thanks to the LORD, for he is good."His love endures forever." Give thanks to the God of gods. "His love endures forever." Give thanks to the Lord of lords: "His love endures forever." to him who alone does great wonders, "His love endures forever." who by his understanding made the heavens, "His love endures forever." who spread out the earth upon the waters, "His love endures forever." who made the great lights-- "His love endures forever." the sun to govern the day, "His love endures forever." the moon and stars to govern the night; "His love endures forever." to him who struck down the firstborn of Egypt "His love endures forever." and brought Israel out from among them "His love endures forever." with a mighty hand and outstretched arm; "His love endures forever." to him who divided the Red Sea asunder "His love endures forever. "to him who brought the Dunkley's family through the midst of it all, "His love endures forever."*

God is our rock! God is our Papa, Glory to Him!

Psalm 18 1-3
I will love you, O LORD, my strength. The LORD is my rock, and my fortress, and my deliverer; my God, my strength, in whom I will trust; my buckler, and the horn of my salvation, and my high tower. I will call on the LORD, who is worthy to be praised: so shall I be saved from my enemies. If Jesus cried out, I too can do so. If Jesus found rest in God, I too can fine rest in Him too. I took a chance on a man named Jesus. And surely he was there with open arms to hold me. He answered my cry! Glory be to the most high!

Readers, do you see how the power of the Holy Spirit worked in my life even without me recognizing it? Yes,

I am now looking at my glass as half full. Tanya could have reacted in a negative manner seeing the outside influences around us and she could have made our lives worst. Tanya could have had the step child syndrome. Remember what I said earlier, my church mother had me on my knees praying before I send the documents to immigration that would "PERMIT" Tanya to be in this country. I need to shout it out loudly, before we allowed fear to consume us, let us learn to "PRAY". There is power in prayer! There is healing in prayer! There is guidance in prayer! I had to write this book to let the world know how great and awesome my God was and is to my family.

I am God's precious child, who was born on November 1, 1964. I was born with a purpose; hand-picked and bought with a price. Jesus blood! Who did I say carried my family? Jesus! He is my tower of strength in my weakest moment. He is my crutch whenever I needed someone to lean on. Equally, my children and husband were bought with a price too. The blood of Christ! How can I say thanks for the many things you have done for me, Lord. When faced with rejections just remember you have a heavenly Father who died for you. That is how much He loves us. You are worthy to be praise!

Taking a Stand

After Colin came home that night, he saw his children crying and I told him what had transpired. He picked up the phone and asked his mother what she had said about not wanting his children, because the children were now crying. His mother said to him, "Is this the first time you see your children crying?" His response was "I have never been rude to you and I will never do so," and he hung up the phone. He turned to me and said, "Yvonne, I don't know my father, he was not there for me and I refuse to leave my children. I want to be there for "ALL FOUROF MY CHILDREN"! I want them not to see me as a father because any man can be a father, but as a DAD. I love you and if we continue to hold each other up, we will make it even if I have to travel the road alone." His siblings did not talk to him for many years to come. They thought he should stand by his mother, because she raised him without a father, even if it meant abandoning his wife and children.

Now let me tell you about this man I called Jesus! Let me tell you about my Papa, Jesus, (as a Jamaican this is ow it gu, mi pupa Jesus walk wit mi). What man puts down God picks up! My father Jesus took special interest in us over the years to come. Thank you Jesus for hearing all our cries!

Psalms27:10 -14 says, when my father and my mother forsake me, then the LORD will take me up. Teach me your way, O LORD, and lead me in a plain path, because of my enemies. Deliver me not over to the will of my enemies: for false witnesses are risen up against me, and such as breathe out cruelty. I had fainted, unless I had believed to see the goodness of the LORD in the land of the living. Wait on the LORD: be of good courage, and he shall strengthen your heart: wait, I say, on the LORD.

Colin quietly but proudly, alone yet boldly, stepped up to the plate to protect and care for his family one hundred percent. This action was enough for his four beautiful daughters to emulate him and to build profound self-confidence, self-esteem, self-worth and self-respect. His lonely walk without the support of his extended family crushed him, but through God's strength, he refused to give up and courageously stood bravely. He was like a lioness with cubs. There were times I needed a babysitter and he would cut his sleep short or put his business aside just to sit with his children. He was very wary about other people taking care of his children. (See Genesis 2:24, Matthew 19:5; 1 Corinthians 6:16, and Ephesians 5:31.)

Colin concentrated on his immediate family. For over twenty years, Colin walked alone, because he chooses to protect and shield his children and wife. For over twenty years, Colin walked alone because he chooses to break this destructive cycle. Life journey is made up of choices. **Joshua 24:15** said, "*as for my house I chose to follow God's way.* For over twenty years, I was lost in a world of my own inability to understand what would make a mother want to isolate her son from a wife who loved him dearly. What would make her not wanting to be a part of her grandchildren's lives? Time would tell and life has a way of taking you places that you had not planned to go. Later on, when faced with my own calamities, I realized victory over bad experiences come only through God. We often see only our own heart's desires and we lack the know-how to help other broken hearts.

I was shattered by the cold behavior of my extended family and mentally unprepared to understand our differences. I was only able to withstand the pressure with the love of God and my husband.

A year later, one morning I made chicken hot dogs for breakfast. My husband said to me in a soft tone of voice, "I don't want chicken hot dogs because I don't like them." I asked him, "Why do you eat it whenever Coleen makes it?" He replied, "My daughter at the age of six is just learning how to cook her favorite dish. I could not hurt her feelings by not eating her chicken hot dogs every morning. I eat those chicken hot dogs with a smile on my face and a grimace in my stomach." That morning I laughed so much. This is just an example of what a great Dad he was and is.

By this time, I filed for my two nephews Oneil and Orrette Flower to attend college here in the USA. My mother was getting older and I felt I needed to take the responsibility of my nephews off her. Even though they were young adults my mother saw them as her little sons still.

Clearly, our outside influence was bigger than us. We had to rely on something or someone that was greater than us.

Colin and I vowed to break this unhealthy cycle.
Over the years, our parenting skills became more rigid because failure was not an option:

1. We started to have daily family worship.
2. We did not send the children to church, I took them.
3. I pushed education and set a standard that "C" is an F.
4. My husband continued to work two jobs and travelled two hours from Brentwood to Rockland county New York.
5. I worked locally, in the town I lived even though I could earn twice the amount of money in Manhattan. This way someone was always near just in case of emergency. I had to be there for the children.
6. The children were enrolled in self-esteem-boosting extra-curricular activities like piano, voice lessons and Girl Scouts.
7. They were involved in community outreach programs like visiting the nursing homes to pray with and for the elderly. Making fruit baskets for

the sick and shut in before they could open their Christmas gifts.

8. I made sure they were on time for scheduled appointments etc. Pathfinders Club, AYS etc.

9. I took nothing for granted; I made sure their homework and Sabbath school lesson were done on time.

God allowed us to experience the rough patches so that upon coming out of them we could tell everyone that it was by God's strength we overcame. We were not the first and will not be the last couple to undergo difficult family relationships. However, nevertheless, I can tell anyone who may be going through a similar situation that trusting God makes the situation more bearable.

Often I hear people say, "There is no manual for how to be good parents," but I am here to let the world know that there is a manual for parenthood. It is the Bible. What a perfect example, in an imperfect world, for us as human beings to emulate.

Genesis 2:24 says, *"A man shall leave his parents and cling to his wife."*

There is one lesson I do tell my young girls. No child ever asked to come into this world. It is by choice that we create children. It is the responsibility of the custodial parent to care for the child whether or not the other parent is involved with the care of that child. Once that child grows into adulthood, we need to allow this child to spread his/her wings with our blessings. That child will make mistakes, but as parents we must be there to catch, hold and pray for God's guidance constantly.

This five percent of my ordeals were written for my readers to know life's journey is made up of sharp pebbles and huge rocks. In my adulthood, I mentally struggled with God wanting to know, Why me? On April 29, 2010 I opted not to ask God, "Why me," because I have come to understand my Papa, God a little bit more and that He takes care of His own. If I just trust Him, He will carry me safely in any trials. My words to you, my readers, whenever you come to a hault in your life look up for direction, listen keenly, because your adversary can drown out God's still voice. Also, stop to smell the beautiful flowers along the wayside because tomorrow is not promised to us.

CHAPTER 5

God's Guiding Hands

Oh, how I learned so many lessons during this time on my journey. I came to understand what the good Bible means in

Isaiah 54:10, *"Though the mountains are shaken and the hills be removed, yet God's unfailing love for you will not be shaken. Nor my covenant of peace is removed,* "says the Lord, who has compassion on you."

Do you know the amount of force and effort it would take to move a mountain? My God is saying that His unfailing love for me is stronger than any demons in this troubled world. I had Yvonna with the guiding hands of the Lord that led me from that abortion clinic. Colin and I cared for our four wonderful daughters and if I had it all over again I would do it the same way. There is nothing greater than when a person can grow to love their partner. There is nothing else out there when one can say, I truly love my partner. I loved my husband wholeheartedly and even though he came with a kind of baggage that he, himself, did not know about, I still love him.

Jeremiah 29:11, *"For I (God) know the plans I have for you, Yvonne,"* says the Lord. *"They are plans for good and not for disaster, to give you a future, hope and eternal life."*

The Lord provided the church family, the Pathfinders, the Adventist Youth Society, the Sabbath School, and the Children's Ministry, which surrounded us with immeasurable love. Most of all, I learned how to relate to everyone through the eyes of God.

Encouragement

The card that I was given, I thought was unjust to me. I found myself working on auto-pilot, refusing to give up. When you have children that are looking to you for direction, there is nothing named quitting!

I realized later in life that I was frustrated, because I still cared for and loved Colin's mother and siblings. My husband would say to me, "Expect nothing from anyone and nothing will bother you. This concept is very difficult to comprehend. At an early tender age, the seed was planted in me that no man is an island, no man stands alone, and that we should love everyone even our enemies.

My counselor once recommended that I simply ignore them and I interpreted this ignoring or lack of expectation of anyone as a form of hatred. To me that is passive hatred. Now that I look at the situation with my in-laws, specifically, their behavior towards me and my children, it became a little clearer to understand. It made sense in human eyes, but I had to answer to a higher calling, to the one who never gave up on me - Jesus. I think hating someone is too easy and gives Satan too much pleasure. The core of my belief is that I cannot hate anyone. The Holy Spirit cannot live in a heart that is filled with hate; but, I will tell you that in order to love someone who you know hates you, it takes divine power; and that is what I prayed for.

I saw how the mighty power of God covered us as a family. All I needed to do was turn to Him completely and allow God alone to fight my battle. My past is exactly what I said, "past, I don't understand it in full, but now I can accept it and move on. My today is my present choice to continue sewing positive seeds in my children, hope that the Lord will work some miracles, and cover the deep wounds that are not yet healed; and I am welcoming a strong future and I will watch the seeds manifest and grow in our lives. I am taking my present with an assurance that God is still in control and a future that I am embracing with hope for a better tomorrow in Jesus' name. That is the reality of my life! I will not give up, give in or quit, because I am blessed to have these four beautiful daughters who God is depending on me to nurture to maturity. A wonderful husband whose love I experience daily. I will do my part and watch God do what He promises. I am moving by faith together with my family towards a brighter tomorrow knowing that God is our rock.

Romans[28] and we know that in all things God works for the good of those who love him, who[J] have been called according to his purpose.

I have hoped that even though God allowed this painful time in my life.

He, God has a purpose for me.
These are some of my philosophies of life which I've tried to instill in my kids and I hope they help you to improve your emotional wellbeing:

1. Do not try to analyze the situation, just love anyway.
2. Make sure you have a song in your heart.
3. Wish everyone well.

4. Respect everyone despite what they may say or do.
5. Most of all, pray for everyone including your enemies.
6. Leave all your worries with God, because he cares for you.
7. Do everything to the best of your ability.

As human beings, whenever we find ourselves in chaos we tend to become fearful. Becoming fearful cripples us from being able to take action. We need to dig deep and look for strength within ourselves. This is the time we need to direct our minds to Jesus, stay on our knees, and shamelessly and unflinchingly stand firm in Christ. Our God specializes in impossibilities. When we are at our lowest moments we need to fuel our painful journey with encouraging words from the book of Psalms. We need to use our trials and experiences for the greater good of mankind and not to inflict pain on others.

Walking Away

Walking away does not necessarily mean you are powerless and giving up. Walking away for me meant the Lord had opened up other avenues for my family to flourish. Somewhere my girls can open their petals and blossom brighter. Somewhere I can find the peace I craved for so over the years.

Colin and I developed high blood pressure and were popping high blood pressure medication. I then realized that in order to have a healthy life with my family, I needed to physically remove our family from the situation. I had to reevaluate the condition I found myself in. I had to find a way to survive emotionally. It was a time during which, even though we prayed, God seemed to be asleep. I would wonder why God did not help me.

As I read the Bible more, I realized that God does not answer all prayers with a yes. Sometimes He says, "No, not yet," because He wants to strengthen us more.

Gold is made through intense pressure and fire; the more pressure, the better the result. God's intention was to build a robust and durable character in me. He wanted me to manifest a strong character that would withstand the pressures of life. Not only enduring and surviving but also emerging with a joyful heart despite my trials. God's greatest intention is for us to live a good, wholesome, upright and happy life while going through our pain. He does not want us to engage in or hold hatred, bitterness, or revulsion, which is the natural behavior of mankind. This is why we have to lean on God totally and not ourselves for understanding.

Proverbs 3:5-6 says: *"Trust in the Lord with all your heart and lean not on your own understanding; in all your ways submit to him, and he will make your paths straight"*. There is a part of us that wants to jump in and do what we think we should do. But my God says He has it under control.

CHAPTER 6

Moving To Georgia

Stepping out by faith

Reinhold Niebuhr says, *"God grant me the serenity to accept the things I cannot change; the courage to change the things I can; and the wisdom to know the difference."*

During my tribulations, I kept talking about moving away and writing a book about my ordeal. Finally, in December 2001, shortly after the calamity at the World Trade Center, I sold our home on Long Island, packed up and moved to Georgia. My husband did not come with us, because he had to work and continue to provide for the family, while I relocated to Georgia and searched for a job. My husband temporarily moved into the rental property we owned in Brooklyn, until he was able to join us.

I felt that I had enough of everything and everybody. I felt I needed to take the saddle off my back that was pulling me down. I finally realized that my surroundings were not healthy for the soldiers I wanted to raise for Christ. For so long, I had searched for life's meaning, enslaved by the words of my in-law, "a mi one mine my children, so send mi son home to me". I decided there and then, I was stepping out of my situation even though I could not see in front of me. I undisputedly claimed victory over my life. For when I met Jesus in totality, He made me complete. I forgot that foolish young lady

I used to be. I walked away with the little sanity I had left. Hallelujah! I had exposed my children to such animosity, to such poison. I walked away with my family with enough faith that God had our back. Hallelujah! I stepped out into a new place knowing God would come through for me! Glory to the Almighty God! Only You God are worthy to be praised!

Leaving was something I should have done long ago. Thank God for helping me to run with my family when I did. My children are now in a happier environment. Thank You God for keeping me, when I almost let go. Glory!

Please, if you are in an unhealthy relationship, especially when children are involved, don't stop to think, RUN AWAY. Move by faith, knowing that God above will take care of you. "A broken child becomes a wanderer. A hurt child becomes lost, and an injured child becomes bewildered".

Let us all take a conscious stand by being activists and protect, nurture, and care for our children. "Our children" means not just those you birth, but the children next door, too. Let us stop ignoring the situation when we see another person trying to put down a child. Studies show that emotional abuse is worse than physical abuse. While the physical wounds heal, the emotional ones stay with you forever, unless one seeks help. So I packed up the children, sold our home on Long Island and came to Atlanta without knowing many people.

The Unique God

When hit by rejection, it is uplifting to know we have a Savior who cares for us. What man envisioned and intended to tear down, my heavenly father above can reverse. He can spin the wheel or turn the situation around to empower you to bounce back to effectiveness after a major setback.

Psalm 139:13-14 *"You are wonderfully and fearfully made"*.

Created by the hands of the magnificent Father called God, you are of a Royal Priesthood. There is none like you in this world or the world to come. You are unique, so at all times ask the divine maker to remind you of who you are.

Isa. 43:2 says: *Though the rivers may overflow and the scorching fire may encroach; you will never be drowned or burned"*

Ask God to be your all in all, so you can change your life by seeing yourself from beginning to end, through His eyes. If we can see ourselves the way God sees us, we would not settle for less.

Rom 8: 31 says, *"If God is for us, who can be against us". We are more than an overcomer"*.

Psalm 27 says: *"The Lord is my light and my salvation, whom shall I fear? The Lord is the stronghold of my life—of whom shall I be afraid?*

Think positive thoughts, claim the love of God, walk in grace, and capture your blessings. Sometimes we need to let go and step out of our situation in order to open new doors for God's blessings to come in.

When I came to Georgia, I also decided that I did not want to work for anyone. I thought I would open a restaurant, because I love to cook and bake. I wanted to become independent of everyone. A few weeks after arriving, I saw a great opportunity in real estate. So I took a real estate class with the help of my husband who would "babysit" in the evenings all the way from New York.

While I went to school in the evenings, Colin would call the house every thirty minutes and talk with the children. He would give them instructions and answer their homework questions and other issues. I successfully passed my test the first time and began a new career as a realtor. Within a year, I had reconnected with Colin's brother's ex-wife and told her about Georgia. By this time, she had gone back to school and gotten her nursing degree. She also looked around in Georgia and bought a lovely house with her three children. God has blessed and carried her with those children.

Things were going wonderfully for us. I was making money, Tanya was in medical school. We found a church to settle in. We were able to take the children on vacation every year and I was able to support my parents in Jamaica.

My children found new friends and were able to adjust in a healthy environment. The younger children were doing well in school, and Colin got a job with a bank and moved within two years. I felt very happy and had a kind of joy in my heart. I felt as if I was not just surviving, but living. My spirit was able to soar to new heights. My soul was at peace and my outlook on life was in harmony with the tranquility I craved. I was in concord with God's words. I would not have asked God for anything other than for me to give back to society and to be able to love my enemies even more. My need to reach out and impact other children was greater than the pain I ever felt when I heard these words, "I don't want your children." I felt an intense urgency to do so. I enrolled in the Georgia Foster Care Program and after completing their training, I kept over six children over an eight-year time period.

In nurturing another child who needed love, I too found the peace that passes all understanding. Restoration began. I felt healing in my soul. I was getting lighter about my situation. As a foster mom, I found that a lot of these children have issues of rejection. My aim was to impact one child at a time, to ignite a powerful, illuminating light in a child's gloomy life. After my first foster daughter left my home, I gave it a rest for a while. I got so involved in real estate that I felt as if I could not devote the necessary time they needed. These children came with lots of issues and required lots of time and demanded attention.

Also, it so happened that around this same time my mother fell ill and I started to make frequent trips to Jamaica to see her. Thank God, with my real estate career I was financially able to take care of her in her final years of life. My brothers and I pooled our resources together, so that she could have the best of everything, twenty- four hour nursing services included. My mother passed away in the year 2005. Rest in peace!

Mission trip

My frequent trips to Jamaica allowed me to see the terrible poverty and needs of my people. I came back with a resolve to help. I made the decision that I had to find a way to give back to people and society as a whole, so I made Jamaica my project.

For every house that I sold I would take a portion of my earnings to different retail stores to buy clothes and food to send to Jamaica. I would clear off the items on the clearance racks and it did not matter the size. I would pack the various items in barrels used for shipping items overseas, hoping one day to take them home and share among my people in Jamaica. One day my friend Dr. Cheryl Samuel came over to my home to see me and noticed the barrels in the garage and she jokingly asked if I was selling barrels. I told her about my special project, she promptly suggested that I expand on the idea by taking it to my church board and getting others involved. I took her suggestion and "the idea exploded" The church board and the church members were very happy to get involved. We all started having social gatherings on Sabbath nights. Each member would make some sort of food (such as fish and dumplings, ackee and saltfish, boiled corn, etc.) and sell it among us and the proceeds went towards the missionary trip. Also, we had another project wherein each person that went to the supermarket was asked to contribute some sort of canned product that could be thrown in a barrel to take with us to Jamaica.

This little seed idea of taking clothes to Jamaica increased exponentially to include doctors and nurses who volunteered to come with us and do free medical screenings. Teachers also came on board in order to take school supplies. Within a six month time period, we had a well-organized, totally voluntary missionary trip planned in tandem with others on ground in Jamaica. The president of the West Jamaica Conference of Seventh-Adventist Church was instrumental in receiving and accepting all the barrels at the Jamaican Customs office at the port of Montego Bay. Thank you Lord!

Some of the poorest areas in Jamaica were in the parish of Westmoreland; so we went and ministered to the needs of one of the poorest communities there. One of the highlights of this trip was when my daughter, Tanya and I, teamed up with other people on the ground and worked in the kitchen serving food to over two thousand people that weekend. It was an exciting and spiritually fulfilling time for us.

Trips like this one prepared me for my present ministry. God trains us and make us ready for bigger things, without even realizing that there was a bigger role/task for me ahead, and now I embrace it without any fear or hesitation, because I am ready.

Today, I am armed with my boots on and my laces tied, my armor and my shield is on and with God's grace and mercy, I have become a soldier for Christ.

I came back from Jamaica with a renewed sense of purpose. After returning to Georgia, I was ready for a different challenge and that was how Tommy came into our lives. I fostered several children, but I would like to tell you about my special Tommy (name changed for the book).

Tommy

It is incredible the things we take for granted in our lives such as family, friends, and love. My first foster child was a teenager. Now I decided I would prefer a younger child who would be easier to mold; since the teenagers come already set in their ways. Having Tommy in our home opened my eyes to how messed up a child's mind can become just from the actions of his own parents and their environment.

Tommy was a special little five-year old boy when he arrived at our home. He was integrated in our home and was totally accepted by my daughters and husband; but his attachment was to me. I could not leave him in a room by himself. He was a scared kid and would follow me around like a lost sheep. I loved him and I told him so constantly. Here is a simple example of this child's fears: if he heard a police siren, his eyes would pop open and you would see terror in them. It turned out that in the home where he grew up; the police were constantly called due to fights within his family.

Tommy was the second of four children born to drug-addicted parents and even with good intentions he was fast becoming a prescription drug addict. In order to keep Tommy under control, he was given heavy-duty drugs such as clonidine, amphetamines, and mirtazapine, just to name a few. My heart bled just watching him swallow the pills.

Tommy visited a psychiatric counseling service twice per month. I had to send at least three changes of clothes to school for him and most days, I had to take additional clothes to school for him. I was so committed to making a positive impact on this child's life that I was a fixture at the school and everyone knew me. I felt so responsible for Tommy. There was nothing I would not go above and beyond to help him with.

When Tommy came to live with us, I took him to church and his entire world blossomed. It was simply strange to me when I bought him suits to wear to church he would say, "I love my costume." He knew that when Friday evening came around, we would prepare for Sabbath. He looked forward to going to church. The Stone Mountain Seventh-day Adventist church offered a full children's ministry and Tommy loved it. The interaction with the other children was somehow different from school.

Tommy saw my daughters as his sisters. My family would take him to Yvonna's basketball games and he would shout whenever she scored, "That's my sister!" From the moment he saw Chadeesia's marching into the auditorium for her graduation from West Georgia University, he would shout "That's my sister!" He belonged to us like no other and he was truly beloved. I recall coming out of surgery, groggy from anesthesia,

and when I opened my eyes the first person I
Tommy standing over me yelling, "Mom you are awake?
I felt truly alive just seeing him.

Since Tommy's parents were drug addicts, he had
major behavioral problems such as ADHD, ADD (my
family called it all the D's). He could not take the school
bus, because he would stand in the aisle of the bus and
refuse to take his seat. The bus driver reported him and
the state made arrangements for a special bus just to
transport him to and from school. Tommy would run out
of his classroom and into the hallway during class time.
I had to come up with creative incentives to keep him
motivated.

The horrible reality of having cancer impacts every
facet of one's life. Tommy was eventually reunited with
his older brother. The state wanted to keep his family together as best as possible. Unfortunately given my present health at that time, I simply did not have the strength
to adopt his brother. I cried for months. My emotional
attachment to him was based on the fact that this child
could have been any of my daughters, especially my
first-born, who was exposed to rejection at the age of
eight. I now know that it is easier to bend a tree before it
takes roots. It is easier to mold a child's life at a tender
age than to fix them later in life.

Tommy took pride in a job well done and I felt great
knowing I was making a difference in a child's life. My
last summer with Tommy, was very special and I'll always
cherish these memories. After my radiation and chemotherapy, I needed new clothes to fit my new body (I had
done a total mastectomy—and had lost some weight).
Every morning in the year 2011, that summer, my church
mother, Mrs. Shaw would come by and pick us up to go
to the mall. Tommy's job was to check each dress price
on the scanner. After he scanned each dress, Tommy

would run over to me with a big grin, then high five and let me know the price for the dress. Initially, the first two dresses he did not understand how to read the numbers but after teaching him, he got it right.

Tommy was just a helpful child, always wanting to help. At home, when I would be cleaning the bathroom, Tommy would get paper towel and try to clean the bathroom mirrors. I realized that this child was different, and that he had grown in the two years he was with my family. He loved a challenge, he took joy in being helpful, and my heart soared to watch the changes taking place in "my son."

This is one of our fondest memories of Tommy. Our family has a tradition of playing games on Saturday nights with friends, especially dominoes. We had a family friend, who would come over to play with us and would talk a lot, so we gave him the nickname "Mr. Chatty Chatty". One evening someone rang the doorbell and Tommy went to answer it. All we heard coming from the doorway was, "Mommy, mommy, its Mr. Chatty Chatty" and we all froze, because the man did not know we had a nickname for him; but, that was Tommy behaving like a normal six-year-old. We realized there and then we had to be careful of what we spoke about around him, because he was like a sponge soaking it all in.

We miss Tommy and every day I pray that I will meet him again someday. The passion that I had for children allowed me to go down the road of foster parenting and allowed me to see the true depths of living with and loving a damaged child.

CHAPTER 7

Restoration

Thanksgiving 2010

After all I had gone through with the total rejection of my in-law; it was somewhat surprising to me that my attitude towards them was always one of love. Over the twenty-year period, I wanted to thank God for guiding my family, especially near my anniversary date. I would periodically call my extended family to say, hello. Yes, and you probably say I am an idiot. I wanted to thank God for taking my family so far. God has BLESSED my family tremendously. To me, it was a milestone. And whenever I take a look in the past and realize how my God kept us sane as a family, it was the least I could do. The more I see the evidence of Christ in our life, the more I needed to get rid of the poison flowing through my body, because my passive resentment was not helping me in any way. So again, one day in August 2010, I picked up my telephone and called Colin's eldest sister. Surprisingly, she was receptive to my call and told me that she had heard about my illness and that she hoped I was doing well. After speaking with her, I immediately called the other two sisters and the reception was the same. His youngest sister and I spoke for a longer time and after getting off the phone, she posted a note on Facebook stating that she was inspired by my strength in dealing with the cancer.

A few days after that conversation, I overheard Colin talking to one of his sisters. He turned and asked me what I was doing for Thanksgiving. I told him I had no special plans. Within a few minutes, it was decided that his entire family was invited to our home for the holidays including his mother. Needless to say, whenever I have anyone traveling to or from our home from a long distance, I would call every so often to find out how the trip was going and where they were and so on. I did not realize that by doing so in this case, they were seeing a caring part of me they had never known before. When his fourteen family members arrived at our home they were truly impressed with where I lived and my family was happy they came. I asked my good friend Carolyn, a great cook to prepare thanksgiving dinner and food for the whole weekend.

We were at peace as evidenced by all the laughter, games, hugs, and a lot of joy. We were on one accord! I know that heaven was brought to earth that day. If anyone had come to our home that weekend, they would not have known that it was the first time in twenty-two years we were together as one family.

One morning, I went into the guest bedroom, where my sister-in-laws were lying on the bed talking. I jumped in the bed with them and somehow the conversation turned to worship. His middle sister asked me, "I heard and saw that you are doing well in spite of cancer. What gave you the strength?" I told them through my past I had learned to trust God and I was sure He would bring me through. I said I wanted to ask them a personal question. They said go ahead. I asked them, there and then, how they could have such a wonderful brother as Colin and hang him out to dry, because he opted to take care of his children and wife---his own family. His middle sister was about to answer when Colin's eldest sister said that, now that she is looking at it, they had been under the devil's influence. She said that was the bottom line of all this friction. They all realized that I was dealing with my illness in a good way, and I told them I found comfort in Psalm 34, which states "*I will bless the Lord at all times, his praise shall continually be in my mouth, through the good times and through the bad times I choose to give God thanks.*"

That morning, my relationship with my sisters-in-law changed. All four of us left the room with one thought that the past was going to be history. We were all intent on going down a new path. One where our children would know each other and be as family should. This gathering was the first time my children met most of their cousins and aunts.

I spoke to my mother-in-law afterwards and informed her that what had hurt the most over the years was when she told me in my kids' presence that she did not want my children. How could a grandmother make a statement like that? I told her that for a person from a Caribbean background, when a father leaves a child, a grandmother is there, and when a mother leaves a child, a grandmother is always the person who is there to catch and put things back together. We cried and we prayed and we decided it was time to heal and move forward.

It is incredible how, with time and experience, one's outlook and attitude toward a problem can change. In my twenties, with no experience, no coping mechanism, I was totally incapable of handling problems, such as dealing with the negative dynamics of Colin's family. However, I can truly say that those challenges and problems mentally toughened me to handle BREAST CANCER. Without those experiences I would not have been ready for BREAST CANCER that had come into my life.

God knows that as sinners, we need to come to Him for redemption and that when we do, it must be with a contrite heart. He is able through His saving grace to give us peace, joy, and love, but we have to ask for it and be prepared to forgive others who have caused us pain and suffering. I thank God for that wonderful weekend; because as a family, we all needed redemption. I know Satan is still raging, but the fight is not between Satan and me. It is between Satan and God.

This is what happens whenever we do not give our life completely over to God and straddle the fence. Satan is not someone to mess around with. He is so experienced. In the summer of 2011, my husband and I went to Jamaica. As usual, my husband loved to hang out with the guys he grew up with. By this time, Colin's mother was retired and living in Jamaica. She would always encourage my husband and me to come and stay with her, instead of going to hotels. While in Jamaica, we went to visit her. Sadly and unbelievably, she started to act unkindly toward me. I tried not to respond and I started to sing the song *"Through it all I've learned to trust in Jesus, I've learned to trust in God."* When she realized that I did not react to her negative remarks, she looked at me and said, "I cannot change my ways, because I am seventy-five years old. I am too old to change." At that moment, when I heard her say that she could not change, because she is too old; every bad feeling, everything in my past came up from the pit of my stomach. I remembered the day she told us she did not want my children. I could hear the children crying. I felt like I was reliving my past; but I was convinced and sure that I just heard Satan talking. It was Satan in the flesh talking to me. With a painful heart, I went to the room, gathered all my clothes and with my mouth glued shut, I left never to return again.

The Bible in Hebrew 12:14 says: *"Pursue peace with all men and the sanctification without which no one will see the Lord".*

My husband could not believe what he was hearing, and he asked her why she was doing this again. Something his siblings and he decided was finished and was thrown into the sea of forgetfulness. She turned to him and said she did not mean it. My husband could not even look me in the face. He was saddened and disgusted to know that through stubbornness, Satan was laughing at us. I was out of there! I left the house recognizing that some people have to be loved from afar and some come in your life for a season and a reason.

I am truly favored by God, because through Him and Him alone, I now can walk away from any issues that have the potential of getting into a quarrel, even when my heart is ripping apart. I can now look beyond my situation and smile at the storm and most importantly, knowing my Father will fight all my battles. I walked away like a wounded puppy, feeling embarrassed. Nevertheless, I was thankful to God for giving me the strength to walk away. That was one of my "victorious moments in Christ". I am learning not to allow others' behavior to disturb my inner peace. I am learning now that I can gain strength from the worse situation. If it does not kill me, it will surely prepare me for the next test. At the age of twenty-two, the human part of me would have just told her what was on my mind, but instead I breezed out of there. Hallelujah!

God wants us to reach that mark, which only can be obtained under tremendous fire. If we are not tested, how would we know through God's strength we can overcome? In my life now, I don't want to just overcome;

I chose to pass beyond the hurt and smile at these situations.

1 Corinthians 10:13 says: *"Yvonne, there is no temptation that can overtake you that is not common to man. Yvonne, God is faithful, and he will not let you be tempted beyond your ability to bear it, but with the temptation he will also provide the way of escape, that you may be able to endure it."*

Romans 14:19 says *"Let us therefore make every effort to do what leads to peace and to mutual edification".*

All the siblings and my family were getting on too well together. Satan had to find the weak link to continue his rampage through our lives. I shed tears writing this chapter of my life. The pain of the past was hideously coming back again. I had been only twenty-two and Colin only twenty-five. We were young, guiltless adults and I felt as though we were paying for the crimes of Colin's father. The load was unbearable for us at times, especially when it was directed toward the innocent, young, impressionable children.

With time, things started to change and I came to grips with my heart's desire. I was finally able to accept some of the things that I could not change. In the summer of 2012, I was with Colin's youngest sister and she started a conversation about her mother. My question to her was why her mother acts so unkindly towards her son's children. She has two grandchildren graduating a few days apart and she came to her daughter's child's graduation, but disregarded her son's daughter's graduation. It is as though her two sons' children are dead. As usual, she sighed. Then she rubbed my leg silently as we were sitting together.

To be honest, her mother's behavior does not bother my children anymore, because my two youngest daughters simply do not know her at all. My first daughter can only remember her in a negative way. I would like to pause here to say something about that.

Out of this distasteful treatment was born a ministry for children. What Satan meant as evil for God's children, God will turn around and work it for the good of those who love Him. Because of the past, I saw how my second daughter, Chadeesia, has a special heart for children. I remember when I was doing foster care; she was living in the city of Atlanta and would come to get her foster brother to take him to church. She has a warm heart for children who are in need; because she realizes that she and her sisters could have been among those children.

We are too firm now in Christ for the malice of others to harm us, but what about other children who cannot fend for themselves and must endure it? This is just outright evil. I told my daughters that the Almighty Father was there for them and that is what counts. For years I allowed Satan to work in my home, building up resentment in me, because of outside influences.   To everyone out there, when you come across situations like this, do not let these incidents define you. Whether you say it silently or aloud, remember, "That's the work of Satan."

Satan's job description is to use anyone and any means to inject pain into people's lives. Just remember to kneel, keep your eyes on the mark, and your mind on God. Worrying does not help the situation it only allows you to create stress, anxiety and prevents you from doing the right thing in your life. It took me years to overcome. Let us leave it right at the foot of the cross. Satan wants to come into my home again, but I tell him, "You can't infiltrate my home, because my Jesus is at the door whenever you knock, ready and waiting." When God is for you, who can be against you? I will continue to delight myself in the Lord.

God said so!

It is doable if we try. In-laws and step parents get a bad 'rap', making people think it can never work, but we can find an inspirational model in the Bible for this. Naomi called her sons' wives and told them, "I am moving from here, because things are not working out the way I envisioned they would. I am going to return to my country and I would like you also to return to your families where you used to live. May God show you kindness, as you have shown me. "All the women cried and hugged each other, because they were such good friends. Orpah didn't want to leave Naomi, but Naomi told her not to worry, she would be fine. So Orpah returned to her family; but no matter what Naomi said to Ruth, Ruth would not leave. "Don't ask me to leave. Where you go I will go, and where you stay I will stay. Your friends will be my friends and your God will be my God."

"Hallelujah!" Ruth followed Naomi back to her homeland, where she worked in the field of a rich man, Boaz, who became her husband. They had a son, Obed, whose son was Jesse, whose son was David. God was blessing Ruth, through the love of her mother-in-law Naomi. What do we know of David? First, he wrote lots of inspired songs that bring comfort to me in my life when I need it most, now many years later, called the book of Psalms. Secondly, he was King of Israel. Thirdly, he shows us that as long as you abide in God, a little man can conquer a big giant. Above all, Jesus came from the bloodline of David. Can you imagine? What if Naomi had been unkind to Ruth her daughter-in-law? What if Ruth had left Naomi, or if Ruth did not accept her grandchildren? What kind of David would we see? Would God be able to say, "David, you are a man after my own heart"? And what if Jesus our Savior had not been born through her bloodline? (See Ruth 1:16). If you have never read this story, please take some time to read it.

I remember when my mother died. Angela my sister-in law called me and said, "I know the cost for burying Mama is enormous. I will take care of Mama's going away apparel." This was not a part of her husband's contribution to the cost. Angela wanted to see that Mama was well-dressed to go off in style. When my brother, Peter's ex-wife heard, she called to ask what she could do, because Ms. Mavis was good to her. Last but not least, my brother, Peter's wife was there in the true sense of the word at the death of my mother and father.

If God did not think in-laws could work, he would not have created the institution of marriage. With God all things are possible. For all those mothers out there who don't believe it can work, take the time to kneel before God and hand the case over to him. When you get up off your knees, you are the example. Start afresh with your "daughters", not daughter's in-law. To those who are already doing their part, continue in the name of the Lord.

For those who have sons and may in the future have daughters-in-law, the key to the in-law relation is to make her your daughter. I guarantee you will have a beautiful relationship with your new daughter.

With all the relationships out there, the key is for us to light our candle, as the songwriter, Christopher Rice said:

Every one of us has a candle in our soul. Let us light our candle and hold it out for the world to see and use it as a guide for their path.

How did we make it?

These are my words now: *"As I went through life's journey, Heaven thank you for seeing our tears, hearing our cry, and answering our prayer. Thank you for sheltering us from the storm and rescuing us after giving it our all. Winter cold has passed and even though we were injured, you saw it fit to keep us sane. Thank you for covering us with your warm hands.*

After all we have gone through, I am eternally grateful to you Lord. Your strength was made perfect in my weakness. Our strength cometh from you Lord, we are strong when we are with you; we will forever look to you. We will always soar like an eagle if we abide in you, Lord."

CHAPTER 8

Making my Dreams Come Through

25th Wedding Anniversary

Colin and I got married in a courthouse in New York. We never had a formal wedding. Life took over and we simply lived. Our twenty-fifth wedding anniversary was coming up. During the time, I was recuperating from my chemotherapy and radiation. Lying in my bed, I really needed a "pick me up." My mortality was first and foremost in my mind. I did not know whether or not I would even live to see another day, and it dawned on me that I really wanted to do a number of things on my 'Bucket List" before I die. So Colin and I decided to have a "real wedding" with a pastor, guests, family, food, bridesmaids, horse and carriage, and the works. As I lay in bed, I planned my 25th wedding anniversary.

Our first decision was where to have the wedding. Jamaica was celebrating its 50th anniversary of independence and my husband wanted us as a family to enjoy the best of both worlds. In addition, Colin is one of the alumni of his primary school who does a fundraising party every other year at the school. In 2012, the alumni wanted to build a computer room and raise funds for computers. So with all these things and events in mind, it was a no-brainer to choose Jamaica as the destination for our wedding.

After the destination was decided, planning of the actual wedding ceremony truly began. We called our girls to discuss our ideas and to incorporate theirs.

Chadeesia, being the more prudent one, wanted us to have the wedding in the US (she was considering the fact that I was still sick and recuperating). However, the decision for Jamaica was unanimous among the rest of the family.

I set about calling my girlfriends, Carol Green and Sonia Brown, and announced my big plans for a wedding. Carol was even more excited than I was about this wedding. Carol worked three days per week and the other four days she was with me, driving me around and taking full charge of the planning and implementation. Oh, to have wonderful friends like these!

We were our own wedding coordinators. I baked my own wedding cake and I even took the time to go to a cake decorating class. While going through this process, I was doing the wedding program when I got an epiphany to write about how Colin and I met and lived happily for twenty-five years together, surviving my in-laws animosity, raising four wonderful girls, surviving cancer and now, glowing in Christ. I decided then and there that this was the right time to start the book I wanted to write all these years. I had a story to tell!

Carol and I decided that we would tackle each item on our list, one day at a time - the clothes, food, decorations, etc. The first challenge was the clothes. While searching on the Internet for dresses, a site popped up from China and we realized we could get our dresses at a quarter of the price if we imported them directly from there. Colin specifically wanted to use the colors of the Jamaican flag as the palette/bridal colors (green, black, gold). The bridesmaids, our daughters, would wear gold and the matron of honor, my sister-in-law Angella Headley, would wear green. The groomsmen would wear black suits with either a green or a gold tie. We got great clothes at a low cost.

There were so many places to choose from in Jamaica for the venue. We chose the Holiday Haven in Runaway Bay, St. Ann. It was new, it had all the amenities of a five-star hotel and the price was within our budget.

Between Colin, our children and I, we had so many friends to invite. We narrowed the list to decide on one hundred family and friends. This was by far the hardest part of planning. We had people in Jamaica and people overseas who wanted to come and share in our happiness, so with a heavy heart we set about deciding who we could not invite. We had decisions to make about the invitations and we settled on basic white. As a matter of interest, my "mothers" (the women who were with me throughout my cancer from diagnosis to treatment) got first priority. There were eight of them, and they all came to Jamaica for my wedding. At this point my state of mind was frenetic. Although my funds were shrinking, my smile was getting wider. Overall, my wedding planning helped to take my mind off my illness.

It was pure joy for me to work out the smallest detail in my wedding plans.

Surprisingly, I spent an inordinate amount of time gathering my friends' names, addresses, and email addresses together. This was definitely one of the things on my bucket list to do, and I felt incredibly accomplished just doing this. I was able to reconnect with so many people.

The travel plans to Jamaica turned out to be a lesson in logistics. Because I was still going through my medical issues, I had to coordinate my plans around all my doctors' visits. My annual physical was scheduled for May; and the wedding was going to be July 29, 2012. I was required to get a full checkup from all my doctors. This list included the oncologist, radiologist, surgeon, and primary physicians. I needed a clean bill of health to travel and stay abroad for ten weeks. This was my challenge. So with grim determination, I made all my doctor visits and thank God they all cleared me to go.

Thank God for the Internet. I was able to do most of my planning and purchase this way; from the dresses, to the cake pans (it was a challenge to get a four-inch pan) and the tickets for traveling-all done online from my laptop---one of the many, great advantages of technology. My wedding plans took over a year from start to finish. Everything that we could possibly need was purchased, packed, and shipped to Jamaica in advance of our arrival. I arrived in Jamaica the first week of June 2012. With eight weeks to go before the wedding, I had lots of things to get done on the ground. I had my trusty friend Carol Green in the United States taking care of anything that needed to be done here.

Most girls or women have a clear idea of what they want their wedding day to be like and I was no exception. I wanted blue skies, lots of sunshine, and of course two white horses with a carriage—yes, a horse-drawn carriage. Again, I searched the web for places in Jamaica that offered that service and I found three locations. I got the best service from Chukka Cove in St. Ann. I also envisioned, seven angels surrounding my entire family, so I got my nieces and my cousin to be the angels.

Included in the items, I shipped to Jamaica, were all the ingredients I needed to bake my wedding cakes. I was staying at a home in Montego Bay and the day I mixed all my batter to bake, it turned out that the oven had only one shelf. Since I was baking over two dozen cakes, I had to call around and found two friends who were more than willing for me to use their oven to bake my cakes. Unfortunately, the original singer had gotten sick and was hospitalized the night before the renewal of vows. Thank God, He is always there for me, one of the young ladies I met while calling around for the oven, replaced the originally singer. It all came together exceptionally well in the end. My wedding was a lesson in "All things work together for good for those who love the Lord."

All my friends planned a wedding shower for me. It was wonderful. During the shower, the electricity went out. We were in total darkness. For some reason, we simply thought it funny and we laughed. The lights came on in a few minutes and we enjoyed the night and went to bed.

With all the planning, praying, and creating, it was time to renew our vows. Sunday July 29, 2012. My wedding day started out beautifully and the day turned out exceptionally well. The horse-drawn carriage was all it was supposed to be. I felt like a princess. My girls were in their beautiful dresses, my family and friends looking happy and radiant... Keep in mind the fact that I had just gone through the most horrible period of my life and here I was living out my fantasy of a dream wedding.

After the carriage arrived at the garden, the grooms-men assisted the bridesmaids off the carriage and down the aisle hand in hand. Then they separated themselves after reaching the Pastor. Now, after everyone was in place, my husband assisted me from the carriage. As with many things in our lives, we walked down the aisle together hand in hand with my long trail sweeping the ground. While we were marching down the aisle, the artist sung this beautiful song, "The prayer" by Donnie McClurkin and Yolanda Adams. This was so different from our first wedding, since we just went to City Hall. Pastor Leroy Daley, the Health Director from Northeastern SDA Conference, officiated the ceremony. I will always remember, when the Pastor asked "Do you take this lady to continue to be your lawful wedded wife. My honey, enthusiastically exclaimed "I do, I do, I do!" Oh how it set the tone for this joyous occasion. We lifted our individual lit candles and lit the third one. Signifying we will continue to be one!

After the ceremony, we took pictures in this beautiful garden that was decorated with some of the most colorful tropical flowers. It was an absolutely gorgeous setting. My dream came true, I was thrilled beyond words. It was awesome!

The reception started out with the bridesmaids and ushers, the flower girl, the angels and then the maid-of-honor marching into the reception. Oh, how I waited for this day. My husband and I marched down the reception aisle to the song 'God raised us up to walk on mountains'.   When we reached at the top of the aisle, the Angels surrounded and made a ring around my entire family, and then the Pastor prayed. It was awe-inspiring. The program began with our children giving their tribute to us. The first person was Yvonna.

Yvonna's Tribute

Children tend to take what they observe and learn in the home and portray it in life. As for me, my parents have set great examples for my sisters and me to follow. The "hustle and be aggressive" attitude my mother has for life, and the hard work and determination of my father, have definitely molded me into the young woman I am today.

In the Dunkley house, education was strongly enforced. The first time I brought home an "F," Dad gave me a whipping, so I would know that bringing home a failing grade was not an option for me. I always remember my mom telling me to finish my education before I pursued anything else with my life, so that I would have something to fall back on. Looking at my three elder sisters, two of whom are Registered Nurses and one who is graduating with a psychology degree; it is safe to say that my parents disciplined us to make education one of our top priorities, which would enable us to find a place in the world so that we could contribute more to society.

My Mother's Kindness

She helps anybody and everybody. I clearly remember when we were vacationing in Jamaica (where else?), and my mom saw a young girl selling books to pay her school fees for the next semester. My mother bought all the books and brought her home for lunch. My life lesson is to share everything; make the best of every opportunity, because it may only come once; and there is always someone less fortunate than I.

Dad

Although my father does not say much, his actions speak louder than his words. In New York, Dad would work two jobs and still have time to play with and discipline all four of us. When my father said something once, he meant it and did not have to say it again. He was always the head of the house. When my mother and sisters moved to Georgia and Dad stayed in New York, he managed to regulate the activities of the home even over the phone. When he finally relocated, we would go to basketball games. I remember going to my first WNBA game with my father. On our way to the game, he thought the tickets were $10 each, but when we got there, the tickets were $160 each. Because he knew I was so excited and really wanted to go, he dug deep in his pockets and paid for both of us. Whenever my sisters or I needed something, whether it was a ride to school or feminine products, Dad was not too embarrassed or too proud to get it for us. My father has taught me a lot growing up. He has led me in the right way and even showed me what the wrong way looks like.

When I think of growing up, my maternal grandparents come to mind as well. I am the baby of them all, so I was allotted special attention. Whenever my grandparents were allocating work duties, I was always skipped, because I was "the baby."

The Advantage of Being the Baby

My fondest moment with Papa was in summer, when almost all of us grandchildren were with him. Papa wanted to go to bed at 10 pm, but we did not want to, so my cousin turned the clock back two hours. Papa came out about 10 pm and said it was time for bed. Well, my sister and cousin told Papa it was not time yet, because it was only 8 pm. Papa went back to his room, then came back out about two hours later and said it was now 10 pm and time for bed. Well, Chadeesia had changed it again to 9 pm. Papa said, "Is my clock wrong or what?" Everyone said, "Yes, Papa, your clock is wrong." Papa came out the third time and said, "I don't care what time your clock is saying, get to bed every one of you, because my clock is saying 12 am, and tomorrow I will fix that clock."

My life would not be complete without those early years with Papa and Mama.

In conclusion, my parents have established great values and morals in each of our lives. So far we have all grown up to be extraordinary, successful young ladies. When we have children of our own, the same discipline, values, and cooking will be handed down to the next generation.

Coleen's Tribute

When I think of my household from when I was an infant to an adult, what stands out profoundly in my mind is food. We always had food in abundance. My mother was either cooking food for one of our birthday parties, cooking for church lunch, or just having an extravagant Sunday dinner and grilling chicken on the "drum pan" in the backyard. Most of all, she would not leave out the potato or cornmeal pudding with the "slushie-slushie" on top. Anyone who knew us knew they could stop by and expect to be full when they were leaving. I never understood or complained about why my mother had to make huge batches of cake or make two or three different kinds of meats for one meal to satisfy everyone's diet (my dad was a "fishterian," my sister was a vegetarian, and the rest of us were meat eaters), though it seemed absurd at times. I realize that it has influenced me positively, because I have grown to love cooking and entertaining people, although on a smaller scale, with food and love.

Another influential factor growing up in my household was education. Whenever my friends came over to my home, they were always grilled by my mother on where they were going to college, if they had taken their SAT yet, and what their occupation would be. My parents strongly encouraged us and other young people to do our best and we knew we had no choice, but to do so. I remember the numerous beatings my little sister would get in school for low grades. As my mom would say, I was afraid of being beaten so my grades were always on the right track. Their numerous speeches about life have influenced me to do my absolute best in my classes. Our parents set the bar and established from an early age that a "C" was like an "F." It was because of this standard, I was able to maintain the HOPE Scholarship (which let me go through college free). My two older sisters have accomplished so much being nurses that I know I have no choice, but to excel in life as well. I am so excited to be completing my undergraduate degree in psychology and to continue on to graduate school. Education has been a major part of my life and I sometimes have to tell myself there has to be other aspects of life to live, too. I love the fact that I have learned hard work tactics that I can apply to other areas in my life besides schoolwork.

Other huge influences in growing up in the Dunkley house are, above all, to put God first in all we do, and never ever break the family unity, "under absolutely no condition." They encouraged us to experience the many beauties of this world while always remembering where we came from. I have made a great and wonderful step and was baptized on Mother's Day, May 8, 2012. Growing up in the church, I learned good morals and to love God and others unconditionally.

Grandparents

Ever since I can remember, every summer, my parents would send us home to our grandparents (Mama and Papa), whom I loved. From sharing with the less fortunate, to having fun vacations, to going to school at Green Pond School, we did it all. When we were sent to our grandparents in the summer, school in Jamaica was still going on, so Mama would send us to school again. She said, "School cannot be too much." These experiences have shown me that there are pleasures after hard work, to aspire to the highest, to leave no doors unturned, and to enjoy success and rewards when they come. I have learned to build an incredible bond with my grandparents, siblings, family, and friends.

My grandparents were exactly what one would imagine a perfect set of grandparents would be like. Even though they thought they did not have enough to give us, to me it was enough. They always cooked, protected, and loved us with everything they had. My grandmother especially, repeatedly told me she loved me, multiple times in a day. It really took a toll on me when she was going through Alzheimer's and experiencing the many illnesses she did. She was an amazing woman, mother, and grandmother. I will forever be her dancing doctor and she will always be my mama.

I am so blessed to be called a Dunkley and I have enjoyed my life growing up with a set of incredible and extraordinary parents. When I was younger, many times I wished they were not my parents, because I thought they were a set of nagging nuisances, but I can safely say now, "I am definitely grateful that wish did not come true." From my father's presence in the home, I have learned how to choose my life partner. My father has always stepped up and been the man in our lives. My mother has taught us numerous life lessons. I would not trade the life I have, not even for a million dollars.

Chadeesia's Tribute

When I think about my childhood, some of the biggest things I remember instilled in me from an early age were God, education, and success. I thought I had the strictest parents ever. We were not allowed to watch TV on weekdays, only on weekends, but we had to go to church all day on Saturday. We had Pathfinders (a church club) every Sunday morning and after Pathfinders, I had piano lessons at Brother Phillip's house. I thought I hated the man. He did not smile, he was a disciplinarian, and we could not play around. Then we had to go to bed early Sunday night so we could be well-rested for school the next morning. By the time I finished the weekend, I had not gotten to watch TV.

I heard a lot of adults say, "I wish I knew then, what I know now." I vowed that when I become an adult, there was nothing that would prevent me from watching TV. Now, I can honestly say, "I wish I knew then, what I know now; I could have accomplished more." Déjà vu! Those "strict rules" that I hated in my childhood have molded me into the respectable, responsible, and accomplished adult that I am. However, I must say, as soon as I got my apartment, I made sure I bought a 36" flat screen TV, so I could watch all the TV I wanted.

Dad

Does anyone know that my dad is a comedian? I remember my dad taking us to the carnival every time it was in town. He also took me to my first movie, Love and Basketball. My dad is a very quiet person, but do not play around with him when it is business time. My dad only spoke to you once, and if he had to talk a second time, he used the belt. He said his grandparents only spoke to him once when he was growing up, and the second time was the belt. His saying now is "yuh bore hole inna yuh ears two different places and yuh still don't listen!" My father has showed me tremendous love. There are so many children out there who, because their fathers did not step up to the plate, are on drugs and have low self-esteem, and cannot build a relationship with other men, because they are looking for love in all the wrong places. Dad stuck with his family through thick and thin, and for that, Dad, you are awarded Dad of the Year in my book. He was the greatest provider. I can honestly say that I have never experienced the light being cut off, not having water, or being stuck in the cold, because the gas got cut off. He has honestly showed me the qualities that I should expect and accept in a husband.

Mom

Wow...Where do I start? Many of you know that we are exactly alike, so we are always bumping heads. My fondest memory is vacationing. My mom loves to travel. It does not matter what my mother's finances were, we went on a vacation every year. When money was low, she would get one of those resort hotels where she would sit for an hour listening to the agent trying to convince them to buy a time share. My mother would get the room that had the kitchenette, and in a minute we had food. No exaggeration, my mom can use twenty minutes to cook a frozen chicken, fry fish, rice, and vegetables, and when she is finished you can lick your fingers and want more.

There are many places we have visited: Disney World, Jamaica, Cayman Islands, Cozumel, the list goes on. Does anyone know that my mom will only eat Jamaican food when she goes out? I remember us spending countless hours looking for a Jamaican restaurant in Orlando. Can you imagine my mother taking us out of a Disney theme park to go and look for a Jamaican restaurant, because she was hungry? Well, my mother went on a quest to find a Jamaican restaurant. It took us hours to find one. While she was driving around in circles, we were getting miserable, so we told her we could eat anything and she stopped at a Burger King to get us some food. To my astonishment, she let us eat in the car and then jumped back on the highway looking for the Jamaican restaurant, because she was going to find it no matter what. Eventually she did. She is tenacious and knows exactly what she wants and she goes for it; she expects nothing less from us.

I definitely acquired the traveling trait from my mother, because I love to travel too. Hence, I am now a traveling nurse. My mother's biggest goal in life is to make sure her children become a positive influence in life; and when all is done, on that great day we will all be caught up with our savior. I believe and hope she knows that she did a great job with her four successful children. Tanya and I are Registered Nurses. Yvonna had a basketball scholarship for school and Coleen graduated in December 2012 with a Bachelor degree in psychology.

Like mother, like daughters. I can say I have the strongest, courageous, spirited, and most giving mother in the world.

The many Jamaican sayings (in patois) that I grew up hearing:

"Pickney Cow don't listen them neck belong to butcher." (If children don't listen they will bear the consequences).

Nuh tell me what the next door neighbor is doing, I'm not their mom. (I don't want to hear what the neighbor is doing in their house, you abide by my rules.)

Yuh want to know why, piglet asked mother pig why your mouth so long, Mother pig said, "You will soon know why, your day is coming." (You are going to learn from your mistake.)

Yuh tink mi an u ah size? (You need to respect me, I am your mother.)

Stick mussi bruk inna yuh ears. (Your ear must be blocked because you are not doing what I told you.)

"Who cyan hear yu will feel it." (Disobedience brings consequences.)

"Nah ramp wid mi pickney, a beat ya till ya soft like porridge." (If you don't quit fooling around I will give you a whipping.)

"You crying, you want sintin fi cry fa." (Stop the noise child.)

This is the best one: when she is whipping you, she would say,"yuh crying, yuh want sintin fi cry fa, (wap again)? Shut up yu mouth pikni!" (Stop yelling before I give you something else to cry for.)

The one question I have is, "Where do you Jamaicans get these sayings from? Let me see hands of all the Jamaican mothers. Yuh di best!" (You are the best).

The biggest thing I have learned from my parents is that the family unit must not be broken—not under any condition. My mother says, "Under any condition, that is a big one you do not break." My parents told my sisters and me that we will make decisions in life that all may not agree with; there will be times when one of us may make a decision that another will not agree with; but respect each other, make your views known about the matter in a godly way; and still be there for each other no matter what. I absolutely love my family. My sisters and I are extremely close. My parents taught me, no matter what life throws at me, put Christ first, be strong, and know that I have a family I can count on.

Tanya's Tribute

"I do not care how poor a man is; if he has family, he is rich" (Dan Wilcox and Thad Mumford). This quote sums up the value system that has been instilled in me since childhood such as the importance of being there for each other; to celebrate together in times of good fortune; and to help each other during times of despair.

At the age of fourteen I came to live with my father, Colin Dunkley, and his wife Yvonne. I remember asking my dad on our way home from the airport, "What am I going to call her?" There are numerous horror stories about "step families," and I did not want that to be me. I remember the first night I walked into the house and there she was, standing at the top of the stairs with her arms wide open. She then said, "Welcome, I am glad you are here." The Lord had brought me into my new family with three new sisters and loving parents.

Mom and Dad, you have always taught me to strive for the best. You both have always been very supportive of my decisions. You also taught me to invest my best in all my endeavors, and to reach for the stars. They have also taught me to have flexibility and to be able to regroup. If something does not work out as planned, I should be able to recognize that, stop, regroup, and try something else to move forward.

They have also taught me to love life and live it to the fullest. Enjoy the "big things" as well as the "small things." They have taught me to cherish even the small blessings and be thankful for everything. Most importantly, my parents have taught me the importance of having a relationship with God and to trust Him even when we do not know the outcome. To be a good witness to those we come across. I was introduced to the Adventist Faith after relocating from Jamaica. This shaped where I went to college and some of the lifelong friends I have met. I remember getting up early every Sabbath morning for church. We were taught to make sure our clothes and meals were ready from the previous day. Most of these principles formed the foundation of my life and still affect the choices that I make.

As the economy took a nose dive, my parents taught me how to maximize what I had and to live within my means. Even now as an adult, I have remained true to these practices. My friends have always played vital roles in my life. Mom and Dad have always been very welcoming and accepting of my friends and assisted them as they could. Some have lived at our house even after I moved away. They are always willing to help and even go above and beyond.

Fun Times in the Dunkley Home

We had some good times in the Dunkley home with Mom, Dad, three sisters, and later two cousins, Oneil and Orrette, who mom helped to relocate from Jamaica to live with us. I will never forget the attic with the Christmas tree.

I can remember clearly, because it was my first Christmas in the USA. I wanted to have a glorious

Christmas. I was so excited having my first Christmas in an adopted homeland. I told my mom we should start getting ready for Christmas early. It was late October, but Mom was not as eager as I was.

So I kept badgering her about Christmas. She told me to go get the Christmas tree and I could start setting it up and when she was finished cooking she would help me. I was ecstatic to get the Christmas tree and decorations from the attic. So I made my way up the ladder and into the attic. I looked around and saw the Christmas tree in the corner not too far from where I was standing. Eagerly, I set out to walk toward the tree, but did not make it far. To my surprise, after about two steps I found myself suspended in midair with one leg through the ceiling of the attic looking at Mom in the kitchen, and the other leg barely holding on. "Oh my gosh!" "What just happened?" Never again will I come back in this attic looking for anything. Unfortunately I did not realize until it was too late that I could only walk safely on the planks and not the plywood. It was a tough lesson to learn.

Mom and Dad, thank you for all your support and love over the years, I wish you both twenty-five more years of love and happiness together. You both have been a good example to me and I will always love you. Over the years you both have molded us into the ladies we now are and I will forever be thankful to you.

Starlight

After the children gave their tributes, we cut the cake. In fact, halfway through the program, the whole place became shrouded in darkness. When we looked outside we saw starlight sparkling, like a beautiful firework display. Little did we know that the transformer on the main street had caught fire: most people thought I had planned it. However, the wedding ceremony continued in the darkness. We had candles and we improvised. We actually used this period to go from table to table to greet our guests and to give out souvenir pictures. Some people were dancing in the twilight and it was in fact a cozy ambience. This was a time when we used our lemons to make lemonade.

My wedding was a true reflection of my life. I am a planner, but whenever Satan throws a monkey wrench in my plans, my Father always comes through for me. The darkness at the wedding did not deter me or my guests; we just saw it as another opportunity to give thanks for everything, good or bad, and to socialize.

In conclusion, I would like to share a poem my husband and I wrote for the tables.

LOVE—our love for each other is a direct result of today's big celebration.
LAUGHTER—Laughter is our best medicine and we are addicted.
SMILE—when we smile at each other it helps release our stress and pain.
KINDNESS—our kindness has deepened our appreciation.

Travelling the World

Like everything else, all good things must come to an end. Having spent ten weeks in Jamaica and having celebrated my 25th Anniversary, it was now time to take Yvonna to college. Yvonna and I boarded the plane home to Atlanta from Jamaica. I prepared myself to take Yvonna to college in Kansas. She had received a basketball scholarship to Cowley Community College where she would be studying Pre-physical Therapy. The school is situated one hour's drive from the Wichita Airport. On arriving at the airport we rented a car, packed our luggage in the back and were on our way to South-Central Kansas, population 12,415.

After leaving the town of Wichita, this one hour ride felt like ten hours as all I could see were cotton and corn fields stretching for miles and miles. I saw no homes or people just horses and barns. Finally, we arrived at the school and with nothing much to do, I unpacked Yvonna's luggage. We went shopping at the nearby Wal-Mart for necessities and then I tearfully kissed and bid her good-bye.

Antigua

After leaving Yvonna, my baby at college, I was not feeling good physically. So, on August 31, 2012 at 10 am, I went in to see my doctor. I did not like the news and I refused to get downhearted or to make friends with Mr. Depression. Right there and then, I looked to Christ and out of this despairing state of mind was born a ministry (Breast Cancer Awareness). The goal of Satan is to destroy mankind by building fear and chaos in one's life. If there was ever a time, I was not going to allow Satan to take away my joy, it was now! I was going to find that little light beaming through all that darkness the doctor told me. I have gone through my past enduring and surviving breast cancer. I was not about to give up on myself.

At that moment, I heard the phone ring and it was one of my church daughters, Nina. I immediately asked her, "What country are you from?"

She said, "Antigua." I told her that I wanted to go there. She asked if I was sure, and I told her yes! She called her mother and her mother said, yes, I could go. My spirit changed instantaneously from sadness to happiness for the opportunity to bring God's good news of how he carried me through my darkest hours.

I told my family that same day and started to plan to start my mission for breast cancer. I am sure I can't do anything about my present medical state, but I can surely help someone avoid it.

One of my daughters asked where Antigua was. I responded that I didn't know, not even where it was on the map, and I didn't know anyone there; but the Lord knows everything and he would open the doors for me. My family and friends thought I was crazy.

This was one of the sanest times in my life. Not knowing was not an issue, because I knew a man who had carried me for so many years through turbulent paths. I have built a rapport with him and without any doubts; I know he had prepared the way for me. Oh what we can do! Where we can go! And the lives we can change together!

That Sunday, September 2, 2012, I purchased a projector. I called in for all my medication from the pharmacy and headed to Wal-Mart to pick up my vitamins. Monday morning I started to pack my luggage. Wednesday night, I called my friend Dr. Cheryl Samuel about 10 pm. I forgot that in order to educate and bring awareness to the people, I had to have information on breast cancer. Cheryl came to my home about 11 pm just for me to have all the slides and to educate me in literally ten minutes. "Amen! Amen!"

With my impaired memory, I jotted down notes so I would not forget. I put my household in order and flew to Newark Airport for my connecting flight to Antigua. I spent the night at the home of Colin's sister. That night we both took out the projector from the box and tried to assemble it. This was an experience for both of us, as we tried to hook up the cables together. The next morning she and her husband took me to the airport to catch my 8:45 flight to Antigua.

While I was at the airport waiting on the flight, a young man approached me and said, "Ms. I have two children on your flight and the airline wants $200 more, because they are under age and the flight attendant would have to take care of them." He said if I would be kind enough to let them sit beside me, their mother would pick them up at the airport in Antigua. Feeling sorry for the man and the two children, I asked whether they had any drugs on them, because I had just survived cancer and didn't want to go to jail as that would be too sad. He said he loved his two children, but school started the next day and they had to be there. I hesitated and then I agreed.

We boarded the plane. When we got to Antigua the immigration officer asked me, if I was related to the children. I told her no, but that someone gave them to me and said that their mom would pick them up from me at the airport. She asked, "Suppose the mother was not at the airport to pick them up, what would you do?" I said, "I will leave them with you." She said, "Lady are you crazy?" She then said that I should go to her supervisor and call the telephone number that the young man gave me. Their mom was there waiting for them. She was so thankful for my help. Now, I did not know who was coming to pick me up. I was in a new country and knew no one.

My God always comes through, especially when you are on his job. Nina's mom was there waiting for me. "Thank you, Ms. Thelma Thomas". We went home and the neighbor, Ms. Junie, a Seventh-day Adventist, had my name on the program for Sabbath at4 pm at Villa SDA Church. Now tell me that I don't serve a risen Savior and it is not faith?

I had to trust my Father, who said in Psalm 50:10, "I own the cattle on a thousand hills". I, God, don't want someone who is prepared; I want someone who is willing for me to prepare them to do my work." That Sabbath I was on the Youth Convention Program at Villa SDA to introduce my ministry.

On Monday, I called a friend of a friend, who was the right connection for everything I could ever want in Antigua. He gave me a pastor's number and told me that he was a very humble disciple of God, and if I called him, he would set me up with every possible person I needed. "Amen!" It was so true.

I called the pastor of House of Restoration Ministry and told him that my mission was to bring breast cancer awareness to Antigua. The pastor asked how he could partner up with me to bring breast cancer awareness to the Antiguan people and asked me to come in and meet him the next day. "Hallelujah"! Before I left his office, I had a 7:45 am show scheduled on Good Morning Antigua, an 11 am-2 pm show on the Observer radio station.

This was my status on Facebook:

"Yesterday I got two links for Radio and TV shows. When I called the producer and told her about the Ministry (Breast Cancer Awareness), she said to me, "Yesterday I was thinking of doing a show about breast cancer awareness." She continued by saying, "from 11 am to 2 pm is all yours on the station." God had these two slots open for me, even before I knew I was coming to Antigua. I was fully booked, each day.

God has a ministry for everyone. We need to get up, stop feeling sorry for ourselves, and move by faith and allow God to open our doors. Glory!

The amazing part of this chapter in my life was that, whenever I went out in the public, whether it was the supermarket, the market, church, or just about any-where, I heard, "Are you the lady that was on the TV or the Radio?" and I would say yes. They would in return say, "Keep up the good work." There were people who actually made appointments for me to do seminars at their churches, because of the shows. I believe the best moment was when I went to the market on Friday, September 21, 2012, and as I passed a stall in the market, I heard a one-toothed man say, "You are the one-breast lady that was on the ABS television show? You are doing a wonderful job! I told my daughters to go get themselves checked."

I felt good knowing that I was contributing and connecting with my people; and even though he said "one-breast lady," I did not feel offended. As a matter of fact, I felt virtuous and trustworthy, because that was what resonated in his mind so he would always remember the effect of the dreaded disease, breast cancer. I remembered the day I was on the Observer Radio Station, and my daughter, Tanya called in on the Radio station program from Atlanta, congratulating me, for the positive step I took to sensitize other families. That day when I heard my daughter on the other end of the phone, my first response was aha aha aha! I was shocked to hear her sweet voice; I was on cloud nine. This feeling was pure joy!

I truly believe that the Lord entrusted us with the task to go tell his people about the everlasting love he has for us, and that he will be there for us when we pass through the water. I did not know I was strong, until I had to be strong. Only if we could just step out in faith, then we would be able to see the powers that lie within us. Only then, we would realize our abilities to move mountains; the capacity to bear each pain, when we are weak. He will give us the wisdom to understand our struggles; if we allow him to work in our lives. And he will give us the appetite to move and function in full capacity when we pass through the rivers. "Hallelujah! Praise his name! He is good!

"Mr. Cancer, you came looking for me and found me. I was minding my own business and you sought me out. Well, I am seeking you out now. You are my business. As long as I live, I choose to make this ministry of breast cancer awareness my business. You were wrong to trouble Yvonne, you are wrong. I am splashing your name across every TV, radio, and newspaper to reach anyone and everyone that will listen to me. Satan, for over twenty years you tried to drive me crazy, but my Father covered me. When it did not work, you tried to kill me. The day that you walked into my life, I told you, "You have knocked on the wrong door." This crisis allowed me to see beyond me. And for that, thank you Jesus.

The Antiguans

Mrs. Junie George is a woman who exemplifies a Christ-like personality; she accepted me just as I am. She is the neighbor of Ms. Thelma, the person who introduced the Adventist message to Nina and Brittany Hill. She came to every presentation that I had at night after work, and I know she was tired most of the time. Nevertheless, she came with me just to make sure I was supported and felt welcome. Thanks to Ms. Junie George.

The President for Breast Friend

Antigua does not have a Cancer Society. It is more of an active support team. When I called Mrs. Eunetta Bird, she was happy to hear from me. We decided to have lunch. She is a warm and soft-spoken person. She speaks of the Support Group with such dignity and with the hope that one day they will have an official Breast Cancer Society. She said this year they broke ground for a Breast Cancer Centre, where they will have the opportunity to treat patients with chemo and radiation. Presently they do chemotherapy at the Mount St. John Hospital and the government sends the patient for radiation to Trinidad.

The government pays for the radiation treatment and the individuals have to find their own accommodations. She said that in November of 2012, she would be going to St. Lucia to visit and observe the Cancer Society, in order to set up the Antigua branch. The Breast Friend was established by a returning resident from England, who survived breast cancer, saw the need for a cancer support group in Antigua, and founded the organization fourteen years ago. Mrs. Bird and I buddied up and did some of the interviews and some of the presentations at the churches at night. She works in the daytime, so she does not have the opportunity to work in this beloved field as much as she would like.

Pastor Stephen Andrews

Upon arriving in Antigua, the St. John's Pentecostal House of Restoration Ministries was one of the first churches I called about the ministry. When I called, I told the Pastor, Mr. Stephen Andrews my name and that I have been a breast cancer survivor for the past year and a half and because of the goodness of Jesus, I was here today to start my ministry about breast cancer. The first words from his mouth were, "How could the House of Restoration partner up with you to spread such awareness to the Antiguan people?" When I heard that, I felt encouraged. I was glowing within, because even though I knew this was a good thing to do, his saying this, motivated me even more. After talking with him, I was more confident in speaking to the next person.

He met with me the next day (poor Ms. Thelma had to take me to every meeting). When I left his office, I had an appointment on Abundant Life radio show and a 7:45 am appointment on the only television station in Antigua. I was very happy and more motivated even though my body was aching a lot. I was very happy to spread the good news of how Jesus carried me through the shadow of death. I went on the show and was able to tell my story to the nation, and because of the over whelming response, the Antigua Broadcasting Show also aired the show on prime time. From the moment I did the program on TV and on their leading radio show (Observer). My life and Ms. Thelma's life changed. We made presentations and did interviews during the day and some nights to the churches. Even though I was constantly tired, I was mentally driven. Sometimes I felt as if I was dyslectic; the words would be in my head, but the hardest thing would be for them to come out of my mouth. I periodically had to sit, because my feet and hands hurt badly. After reaching home, each day, my body was exhausted; I would sleep like a baby in the night from fatigue. Nevertheless, it was worth it. Lives were changed, people were more knowledgeable about the disease of breast cancer, and people made appointments for their mammograms.

Two Churches That Stood Out:
The Faith of the Wesleyan Church

A day after being on ABS Good Morning Antigua, I got a call from a lady who had gotten my telephone number from one of the shows. She said to me in a high, boisterous, overexcited voice, "Are you the lady about breast cancer awareness?" I told her yes, and she said she had just called her Pastor to tell him about me, and told him that he needed to have a church meeting for me to talk with his members. She said that the message was profound and that it hit home, because I was a breast cancer survivor and because of the way I proudly introduced myself with confidence and with pride in being a breast cancer survivor. She asked if I could come next Tuesday to her church. I told her, yes and she was very thankful.

The following Sunday morning the Pastor called me at home to get more information on me, because he was going on the radio station to promote the meeting at church, and to let them know that Mrs. Yvonne Dunkley would be at the Faith Wesleyan Church in All Saints on Tuesday night to bring breast cancer awareness to his church. They sent someone to get me from home, and upon reaching the church, I was greeted and welcomed by a packed church. "To God be the glory". The people were very engaged, stimulated, and happy, and had many questions to ask. Some planned to call and make appointments for a mammogram. One of the things that stood out in the pastor's mind was the faith that I had in stepping out and allowing God to captain my ship to spread the word. When I left the church, I was glowing and full of high spirits, because I had been able to reach people that night. "You are awesome, my Father".

Melt in Fire Tabernacle Church
I also got another call, similar to the one above. A lady called me in a concerned and anxious tone of voice. She asked if I was the person on the Good Morning Antigua Show, and I told her yes. She said, in an uneasy tone of voice, "I need you to come to my church to talk on that issue (breast cancer awareness)." She said that she had spoken with her pastor and they wanted me to come, so would I please not take any other appointments for that night. Right there and then, I knew

something was going on at that church in reference to this disease, and that someone was very concerned. I felt if my presence would help, if I could hold someone's hand, then my life was worth living. You see, this mission is not just to educate and bring awareness to people, it is also for me. I will also feel healing within me.

If we can see this disease for what it really is, we would make more conscious decisions about our life such as eating healthier foods, making our mammogram appointments, doing clinical appointments and self-exams, looking for retracted nipples and a red rash on the breast. We would also take it a step further, to encourage someone else, whether it is your neighbor, niece, cousin, or sister, to be more vigilant and pro-active about their health.

I met so many intriguing and sweet Antiguan and Barbudian people. I did not know so many Jamaicans live in Antigua.

I am happy that people could identify with me. I even met some relatives of the Dunkley family at the St. Johns SDA Church and how can I forget my girl-friend Sandra Knight sister Dimple. We attended the Northern Caribbean University together, and when I told her about going to Antigua, she called her sister there and told her to welcome me. Dimples, her sister, and her niece, who are Jamaican, took me out to see the Heritage Centre where the cruise ships dock in town. While we were there, I saw guineps, a fruit that I love; and I bought a whole lot.

On September 29, 2012, while I was getting my ticket from the agent at the airport, I was greeted with warm words. The immigration lady told me that she had called the various churches to come to a presentation, but had not been successful, so I must come back. I did not know I would be this energized and galvanized about giving someone information.

I came back home during the time of Breast Cancer Awareness Month. This month brings back memories. Memories of chemotherapy, my port being cut without explanation, of turning 46 years old and feeling as if I wanted to 'give up the ghost'; but then another part of me was able to emerge from within.

When I left the United States of America on September 8, 2012 to go to Antigua to start God's ministry about breast cancer awareness, I had no clue of whether I could reach even one soul. Yes, I did. My aim was to reach one soul and in turn I touched more than half a country. The potential and oomph that lies within one soul, if we allow Christ to transform us from the inside is imaginable. Out of my struggling life was born a ministry.

Trip to Europe

Breast cancer has given me a new perspective on life. When you are afflicted with a disease that has a life expectancy of between five to ten years, you want to cram life in, live life, enjoy life, wake up and smell all the roses. Sleeping seems like a waste of good time when there is so much to do in so little time.

My God, they say looks out for "idiots and little children". Well, I am not a child, so I must be an idiot, because he puts things and people in my way that simply serve to enhance my life. My daughter Coleen is dating a nice young man, who works with an airline, and he was gracious enough to give me another buddy pass; just what I needed.

My eldest daughter Tanya wanted to celebrate her thirtieth birthday in Paris, specifically at the Eiffel Tower. She asked me to do it with her, so I set about planning a one-month trip to Europe. I had never been to Europe, and this also, was on my bucket list.

It was an election year in the US, and I wanted to vote before I left the country. I was one of the first persons in line for early voting in Georgia. Tanya had only two weeks' vacation time, so the other two weeks I had to spend alone. My flight to London was wonderful. I took my medication, which included a sleeping pill, and the flight attendants only woke me up to eat during the eight-hour flight. It was smooth sailing while I slept. I arrived at London Heathrow airport on October 15, 2012. I knew no one as I was starting my adventure. There was an aunt, whom I had never met, but I had gotten her number from my family and when I called her from the US, she told me, "You are family and you can come and share what little we have." She and her husband met me at the airport. It was wonderful to meet relatives that I never knew. They took me home via the train, and they showed me nothing but love for two days.

Two days after I arrived in London, I went to the airport to meet Tanya to begin the second leg of my adventure. We went to a small, beautiful hotel in London, where we stayed for two days. I must say that between the trains and buses, the transportation system in London is very efficient and easy to navigate. Initially, It was difficult for me, because of the short-term memory loss from my illness, but Tanya was there to handle the directions for us.

Tanya and I visited the places that tourists are encouraged to see, such as the Tower of London, London Eye, London Bridge, Big Ben, Westminster Abbey, House of Parliament, Trafalgar Square, and Buckingham Palace, to name a few. The sites that we hear about while growing up turned out to be more exciting in reality than in the books. I actually walked on the London Bridge, that we sang about when we were children. It was almost surreal.

The weather in London was cold and dreary, but our spirits were high, so we ignored it. We bought hats and other knick-knacks to take back for the family. The difference in language is incredible, even though we all speak English. One example was when I kept asking the customer service representatives at the train station if there was an elevator, they kept telling me no, they had only "lifts." Little did I know they were talking about the same thing. I found it hilarious when I finally figured it out. I traveled on the three-wheeled tricycle and I ate lots of British fish and chips. London with Tanya was a great adventure.

Our next stop was Brussels, Belgium. I can truly say this country is one of the most beautiful in the world. Unfortunately, we spent only one day there. My impression of Brussels is that it is the perfect place to retire. Surprisingly, the nights there seem like day and all the elderly couples were out in the open air, sitting on benches eating pastries and ice cream. It was an incredible scene. It is one country that I would love to revisit.

Tanya and I took the Eurostar (the electric train) to Paris. I believe that city is totally overrated and expensive. We arrived in the City of Lights during the night. When we got to the hotel, they informed us they had no reservation for us. Imagine being in Paris with nowhere to sleep. For some reason, I did not panic. While poor Tanya was trying to resolve the situation at the front desk, I was on Facebook talking to my family and trying to work out the situation with our booking agent. It was Fashion Week in Paris and all the hotels were booked solid. Wanting to see if the booking agent had sent her a note, Tanya looked at her e-mail after talking with the front desk person, who had decided to allow us to sleep in the lobby on the sofa (at least he was being nice). Tanya found an e-mail that an old friend from primary school in Jamaica had written to her to let her know that she was living in Paris. "Wow, was this for real?" The thought alone, that a friend she had not seen or heard from in over twenty years, had just got her e-mail address from a friend back in Jamaica. God just showed up at the right time! Can I say, the God I know now, He does not always show up when you want Him, but surely, He is an on time God?

This is how my God works miracles. John 6:6 states, "Don't worry about your present situation, God already knows what we are going through and He has already taken care of it." We called Tanya's friend, who promptly invited us over to her apartment (flat), where we all merrily slept on a single bed. Yes, all three of us held on a single bed in a 16x16 studio apartment.

Early the next morning, she took us to a small motel, which turned out to have a communal bathroom. This seemed to be common for most of the motels in that area. Imagine that Paris, the place that almost every person wants to visit, has a communal bathroom, something I had never heard about. This was my worst nightmare, because I take my medication at night and I go to the bathroom throughout the night. I genuinely felt fear at that motel, and irrational though it was, I would wake up poor Tanya every time I needed to use the bathroom. She would stand outside the bathroom door while I used it. We had to live through that for three days and even though it was the worst, it totally embodies life. You learned to live within your limitations, instead of making a major display out of the situation.

Our first Paris tour was to the Palace of Versailles. That building is huge and beautiful; that is Grand Paris. The gardens were breathtakingly, awesome, and it took us half a day to complete the tour. We had to experience some sort of shopping in Paris, but at the mall we went to, a simple scarf was being sold for six hundred Euros. Wow! We ended up buying something anyway, a little plastic pack of spices for twenty Euros. All of a sudden, the United States of America appeared to be a wonderful place to live in terms of the real cost of living.

We went on the double-decker bus tour that ended at the Seine River. It was cold, yet exhilarating. Tanya, actually made it to the Eiffel Tower for her birthday; which was a dream come true for my daughter and me. Thank God, I was there to celebrate the occasion with her.

Our next stop was Rome, Italy. The hotel we stayed in was much better than where we stayed in Paris. They had all the amenities we needed, including Internet service. We visited the Vatican, where the line was interminably long. It took us an entire day to do that tour. The Sistine Chapel was worth the wait; to see Michael Angelo's work of art is awe-inspiring.

After leaving Rome, we went to Naples. This represented rural Italy to me, and it was interesting to say the least. Similar to our experience in Paris, the booking agent had again not made the reservation for us. Fortunately, a friend of my daughter lived in Italy and he came and took us to his place on the US Navy base, where they had a lovely hotel. Again, my God worked things out for us in the middle of the night.

The following morning our friend took us on a tour to Pompeii—that is old Italy. We went through the ruins of the city. From there we went to Sorrento, which is wine, olive oil, and family country. The next place on our adventure was Venice, the land of water.

When we arrived at the airport, our luggage was over by eight pounds. We would have had to pay one hundred Euros for the overage. Tanya got the brilliant idea to take the overweight clothes out of the suitcase and put them on. By the time she was finished layering her body, she had on over four leggings, two pairs of pants, and tops. The downside to that situation was that she could not breathe. The two-hour trip was stifling for poor Tanya, and imagine having to do that coming back as well. We started out on an adventure and we sure got one.

I got to Venice, the land of water. Most of Venice's transportation activities are done by boats. Everyone seems to own a boat: the garbage system, the mail system, couriers moving parcels from one location to the other is all by boats. The emergency system, such as the police, ambulance, fire, and even hearses, are operated by boats. It is beautiful scenery seeing the gushes of waves splashing as the emergency ambulance races by. Venice is exactly the way I imagined it to be.

What a beautiful sight to see different merchants lined along the water selling various souvenirs, and the café shops with their inviting cookies and ice cream. We bought souvenirs and exchanged birthday gifts there. We went to a diner to have lunch. After sitting around the table, the waiter told us we had to pay extra in order to be seated. Some of the tables and chairs are actually in the water. We were hungry so we paid up. There is a famous quote that says, "When in Rome do as the Romans do".

The scenery of the gondolas carrying relaxing tourists is simply breathtaking. The gondolas even have an entertainer to play soothing music to the tourists as they sight-see, sailing down the Grand Canal. The amazing thing is that this whole city is on water. We stayed in Venice for two days, and that part of our adventure was totally inspirational.

Tanya and I left Venice and flew back to London in more clothes than she initially wore there. Remember, she had already stuffed six pounds on her coming to Venice. All the souvenirs and goodies we bought in Venice, my sweetie pie. Tanya had to stuff them on, so we did not have to pay the overweight. She survived it and now I am telling the story. I thought the English pound was too much, but then we found out the euro was even more. The countries that used the euro do not accept the pound.

My conception of England was in total contrast to the reality of England as I experienced it. The apartment buildings were small, drafty, and uncomfortable. This was old country. Now I can fully understand the reason why when Jamaicans go to England, they return to Jamaica and build these big homes. They spend their years in England being claustrophobic. I stayed with Debbie Oneil for over a week and I enjoyed my stay and celebrated my birthday with her at the Westfield Mall. Debbie you are such a sweet person!

I was more than surprised that after twenty-five years, when I finally was able to travel all over, my husband kept insisting that I come home, because he was missing me. I was not sure what was happening to him, but I certainly appreciated the fact that he missed me and I was wanted back home. Sometimes we need to be away from our loved ones. I returned to the US after touring Europe with much fun and laughter. I found myself so blessed to even have more fun and a passionate romance awaited me. It was as if I was dating all over again and I knew it was time for me to be home, because it was two weeks before thanksgiving. My European adventure was GREAT!

CHAPTER 9

God's Name must be lifted up

Stepping Out

Thanksgiving 2012 was my first Thanksgiving without all my children. Chadeesia is a travelling nurse, so she is travelling the United States while getting paid. My baby, Yvonna, was at school and did not get a break, because of basketball practice and games. My Coleen was off to Connecticut to go to a wedding with her boyfriend and so Tanya would be the only daughter home. The week before Thanksgiving, I got a telephone call from Brooklyn from a very old acquaintance I had not seen in over fifteen years. She said my pastor's wife gave her my telephone number. She wanted to find somewhere in Atlanta for her daughter to spend the night. The day after her call, I had another person call from Texas to say that she was coming for Thanksgiving. I was blessed to have the two families to share Thanksgiving with me.

On December 17, 2001 when I purchased my house, I pledged to the Lord that I would use this home for the good of mankind and praise God that is exactly how I live. Whenever people stop by they must feel the presence of God in this home.

Well, it so happened that my new daughter, we will call her "J", stayed longer than they thought she would. As a matter of fact, she left to visit her mother for a few days and then came back to my home before going off to college.

I am about to tell you how my God worked out my calamities. I was struggling with writing this book. I felt God was not there for me. Only later did I come to know that He was right there carrying me, when he could only be seen in Colin's and my footprint in the sand. *"God you used this period of my life to scrub me shine, build up my faith in you so I would be untouchable when breast cancer came knocking at my door. Thank you for making me strong for today, my present."*

While my new daughter was with me, she went to church. While she was there, I saw her send out a Facebook status, which read: "I now know the meaning of 'going to church with a heavy heart'. Praise God it's the best place to be when you're hurting. God only knows". When she came home, I tried to encourage her. She left on Sunday, November 25th to go home to North Carolina. On Friday, December 2nd , she stopped over for the weekend again before going to college. She was so sad, she kept to her room, and I tried to cheer her up.

While we were talking, she found out that I was writing a book. She immediately said that she wanted to write one, too. While I was talking with her, my insides were tearing apart, because her story was too close for comfort. I was seeing how, if I had not grabbed the bull by the horns, stood up and moved away, this would have been the experience of my children. Her presence was sending mixed feelings to me. I was happy she was there, but dying inside knowing that this could have been Chadeesia's experience. We decided that she would have a paragraph in my book.

Now, my readers, I had been writing my book during the time I was laid up in bed recovering from my illness in 2010. I have never spoken to this child. The last time I saw this child, was about fifteen years ago, so that would put her at age five. I had not seen her mother all this time, either. The huge struggle I was having at this moment was whether I should publish or broadcast my past, because others might feel uncomfortable about the book. My story was not like hers, because my husband stayed with us as a family. Nevertheless, if my husband had left us to go home to mother, if I had not jumped on the emotional issue that my children were going through at age eight, if I had not, yes, if I had not... This is my point: the end result would have been the same broken children. This is why I said that your story may be different from mine, but if we allow our children to be broken and stay broken, what a world that would be. The children do not want to carry the burden of our marital issues. They just want to be children. We as parents need to figure out the situation before it spoils our innocent children. We need to stop thinking of ourselves.

And here is my new daughter J's story. It's from the mouth of J, from the broken heart of J, from the shattered mind of J, from the child who thinks she is beaten down from the cares of her parents.

No one ever considers the children when adults are going through hard times. My name is J. I am twenty years old and I am the product of a loveless marriage. Some might wonder how that happened, but it is quite simple. The problems don't just randomly appear one day. They are always deeply rooted. Only God knows where my family's problems began, but there are issues on both my mother's and my father's side that have prevented them from having a successful marriage.

As a child, life was enjoyable. I was always around both parents, and I had the niceties of life plus a little bit more. Things began to change when I found my mother crying about my father one night. All I can remember is my mom saying, "Why couldn't he just be faithful!" My mother loved my father and because my brother and I were still young, she never left him.

Years and another romantic affair later, I find myself living in a house that was meant for four, but is only occupied by three. My father never moved with us when he and my mother decided to leave New York. We had been living in North Carolina for six years when my father just started coming to visit less and less. While I was in college in Alabama, he only came when I was home. Today my parents are divorced and my mother is hurt. My father refuses to admit his faults and is remarried, while my brother and I have found our own way to cope. I have found myself doubting God and doubting the very sanctity of marriage, as well as my desire to one day become a loving wife and a compassionate mom. The problems I have had have caused me to look for love in all the wrong places and to chase after the wrong men, and I have even found myself being a victim of sexual abuse, all because my father left. I have been the product of a loveless marriage for twenty years and not a day goes by where I don't pray that God will help me break the curse.

Some days I am positive, while others I just want to be locked up by myself. I've experienced many things that I shouldn't have, and endured my parents' lack of love in the home, but my God is faithful to me. Where my father was lacking, God made up and more. God consumes me with His love, and guides me like a real father would. He pursues me and corrects me. I am learning from my parents' mistakes about what makes a marriage, but it is God who teaches me how to love selflessly. I am nowhere near healed or whole, but I am finding my way to the path that leads me there".

What Makes Me Cry?

The day that I received this letter from J, I was just cry-ing uncontrollably as all the old feelings came back. My nightmare of a broken child was being manifested in a child who was visiting my home, whom I had only known a week. My heart started to race; my head began to feel as if it was going to break in two, and I found my-self shouting out loudly, *"Lord where were you? Where were you when this child needed you? Lord, show up Lord, Show thyself in my daughter's life. She needs you this moment!"* I literally cried myself to bed. I did not get out of bed for about three or four hours, until I heard my telephone ringing. I thought I was being purged while writing this book. I thought I was emptying all the unre-solved feelings. It was at that moment, I realized, that my healing process had only just begun. Friday, December 7, 2012, I decided to write another book before I die. It will be about J. "What About the Children?"

There is nobody in this world more optimistic about life than I am, but all of us will die someday. The good thing about mine is that I got a second chance to live, and I am cherishing every moment. My Lord has too many things for me to do here on earth. The Lord has entrusted me with much, before I go home.

After reading my new daughter J's letter, I now know there is another world out there with broken children from broken homes, who are crying out for help. We as par-ents are too busy licking our own wounds. Meanwhile, the children live in such darkness, which is beyond their little brains. Some act out in unhealthy ways just to get attention. Parents! God entrusted us with these children. Stand up for them, even if it means putting yourself out in the cold. That is all I have to say this moment, in the name of the Lord. Meeting my new daughter was ab-solutely not by chance. She was directed by the Holy

Spirit to my home. If I had any reservations about writing this book, especially the latter part, now, I am surer than ever. Some people are living in a bubble, hiding away from reality.

Sometimes I could not address the issues, because I was sinking. I had to go around issues. I would tell myself, I will deal with it another day. There are only twenty-four hours in a day and it seemed as if my twenty-four hours were already full and running over. I had to bury some of the hurt deep down just to get by. I can tell you, when it came to decisions about my children, it was a no-brainer.

Standing for nothing in your life means that you will accept anything even if it goes against your will.

My children came first. It did not matter what situation I found myself in, what pain I was feeling at the time; my children came first all the time and every time. The book is done! The chapter is closed! It is one thing to answer to the children later, why we as parents were not there to cushion the pain, and it is another thing when we have to answer to my God. I will have to give an account for mine, and also for yours if they were within my reach. They are all our children. They are all God's children. I could just picture Chadeesia's mouth asking me why I was not there.

They are first in my life at all times and in every situation. We need to listen to our inner voice and stop putting men, grandparents, women, and anything that might sidetrack you from being there for your children, ahead of them. I will never ever forget my husband's words on that gloomy day, when I packed his bag and said, "Go, your mom just told me to pack you up and send you back to her." He said, "I don't know my father.

He was never there for me and I refuse to leave my children." He said, "If you want to leave you can do so, BUT I will never leave my children. Now, if we stand together, if we unite together and hold each other up, we can make it." I am very proud today to say that I am stronger and, wiser because my husband stood with me. The link was unbreakable. We had no choice in the matter, our children came first. We have learned from our mistakes. As the children said, because of our actions they now know what to expect and what not to tolerate in a relationship.

My husband is my life partner. The greatest thing about my ordeal was that my husband and I got extremely closer and, an indestructible and indissoluble bond was formed out of our pain and our life's struggle. We were and still stick together like glue. He does not talk much, but I can read his silence most of the time. He is an extremely private person, who lives with a social butterfly. Two total opposites, yet meticulously anchored within. The thing that we have in common is our love for God, respect for each other, and bringing up some well-rounded ladies. This relationship was glued through our heartache, in wanting to see the children succeed and not have psychological problems later in life. I am looking forward to the Breast Cancer Ministry tour that both of us will be taking to Jamaica for ten weeks.

He will be assisting me by setting up all the equipment, and at the end of the seminars he will be marketing the books and setting up appointments. With all of my disabilities he accepts and wants more of me, and I want all of him. *"Lord, thank you."*

Something positive did come from this awful disease of breast cancer, a ministry. I would like you to think about my blessings. I am content and happy with him and he is satisfied and happy with me. Put them together, you have both of us intimately in love. In the end the Lord worked all things for good for those who are called for his purpose. I will be touring the world to do something that comes from my heart; pursuing the ministry with my husband right beside me. After a long day of doing seminars, I get to go to bed with my husband beside me in different countries. Could I want anything else besides? No! There is no way I could regret my past.

It is my past that took me to where I am in life today. A few years ago, I had no clue where I would be in my life. Hallelujah! Hallelujah! My God is able to transform life, to heal any open wound, bind any pain, reconcile any issue, restore peace, make good on his promise, heal any sickness, mend any broken relationship, and repair any shattered heart. The key to this promise is total surrender of one's self to God. We can't be saying, "I am too set in my old ways, or I am too old to change." God says it does not matter where we are in life's journey, he can restore you and use you for the good of others.

What Are My Darkest Moments?

As a breast cancer survivor, I have to see all my doctors and have my body checked often. I am human, so I have the tendency to be fearful. Whenever that feeling comes upon me I just look to God and have a little talk with Jesus. In Christ I can find light in every situation and it does not matter how dark it may seem. I have come to realize that most of the time we are afraid of the dog without even looking to see if the dog has teeth. We allow fear to make mountains in our minds, until it cripples us and drives us insane. Fear and faith cannot live in the same house. I cannot continue to say I trust God and another part of me is saying, "I am afraid."

I am no longer living in fear when I can look to Christ in every aspect of my life. I have thrown myself into the book and the ministry and this distracts me from myself. I refuse to nurse my problem or feel sorry for myself. The Lord said, "Yvonne, my grace is like a lantern in your darkest hours." He said that his grace is enough for my weakness. "Hallelujah." How can I be afraid? God bought my freedom a long time ago: I cannot entangle myself with Satan.

Galatians 5:1-4 says *"I have freedom in Christ, so Christ has truly set us free. Now make sure that you stay free, and don't get tied up again with Satan."*

Romans 10:13 tells me that *"whosoever calls upon my God shall be saved."*

My duty is to call upon God when I am surrounded by darkness. God is the flashlight whenever I find myself in the tunnel or in the pit of circumstances.

How is my Health Now?
I was diagnosed with HER2-negative which is an estrogen driven breast cancer. I take 1 mg arimidex, generic anastrozole pill once per day. I have problems walking or standing for extended periods of time. The side effect of the anastrozole is an aching muscle pain, which makes me feel as if I have arthritis. I happen to have neuropathy on my right side. Because of the neuropathy, I have a burning, shocking sensation on the side of my leg. My extremities are either numb or tingle twenty four hours a day. My fingers lock on me; I cannot move them at times. My legs burn whenever I walk, stand or lie down. One of the side effects of the chemo was impaired memory. Also, nineteen lymph nodes were removed from my armpit, so, I am not allowed to

lift anything over five pounds. Lifting anything over five pounds would result in lymphedema.

I am always feeling weak despite the extra iron I take. Every morning my husband juices fresh green vegetables and makes a fresh fruit smoothie in the evening for me. I try to stay on the healthy side of life. In spite of all my disabilities, I am determined to push and do my utmost to enjoy life and not just exist or live on auto pilot. I want to see more of the world, count my blessings, strive to new heights, sensitize women about breast cancer, wear my smile all the time, delight myself in God's glory, and most of all give God all the praise.

What Makes Me Smile?

There are lots of reasons why I smile. Smiling comes naturally to me. It is part of my persona. My other mother, Mrs. Hazel was always asking me why I always smile even during serious stuff. And people are now telling me I look younger than my age. In the last set of family pictures I took, everyone asks who is the mother. I refuse to wear my problems on my sleeve. Studies show that smiling relaxes the muscles in the face which makes you look younger.

I have made a vow to myself to continue to keep my focus on God. There are many things that will happen in the future that I will feel I cannot face. However, as a man I met in Antigua named Mr. Terrific (C. W. "Terrific" Roberts) said, "Keep your focus in the spirit realm for there is health, healing and wholeness therein".

"Thank you Jesus!" I have now started the Breast Cancer Ministry and like any other business out there, I will need funding. I know that God will not lead or entrust anything to me without having prepared the way first. Over the past week, I decided to make a schedule for the ten weeks I will be in Jamaica with the ministry. I was

having a little challenge with getting Sunday Churches to present the seminar, so I Googled Sunday Churches and media to tell my story. After a week of working on the schedule, I was encouraged and motivated by everyone I spoke with.

Here are some of the responses I received that made me smile:

Re: Breast Cancer Awareness/ the Church of God Universal Church/March Town/March 3, 2013

Dear Mrs. Headley-Dunkley,

I am responding to your generous offer to visit the March Town Church of God (Universal) on March 3, 2013 to do a cancer awareness presentation. This offer has come at a timely moment as we are faced with a serious challenge. I have been praying for such an opportunity, as I believe the community as a whole needs to be educated on this health issue.

I am convinced that your offer has been made in answer to prayer; but then we serve a mighty God who specializes in things thought impossible, and there is absolutely nothing that He cannot do.

I hope to be able to announce a time that I can use for this meeting. Since we normally have a 5:00 p.m. session with the young people we are thinking that time could be used for this purpose.

Also, I plan to invite representatives from other churches and other groups in and around the area to share in this session.

Isn't it amazing that we pray in one location and God answers in another place so many miles away? What a mighty God we serve!

I felt so touched when I read of your promise to God to spend the rest of your life ministering to others of His healing powers. Thank God He has not lost His power. He is the same yesterday, today and forever.

May His blessings be forever yours. Praise the Lord!

God bless you and your dear husband for his love and support.

Hoping to hear from you soon.

Pastor Enid Jones

Yours in the Master's service

I called a Sunday Church I found on Google. I recognized this Church instantly, because I remember that as a child I had to pass it on my way home from school. I dialed the number and said to the receptionist: "My name is Yvonne Dunkley and I am living in Atlanta, Georgia, and I am a breast cancer survivor. My pain of dealing with breast cancer has borne a breast cancer ministry. I am visiting Jamaica for ten weeks to bring awareness to the people, and I would like to secure a time with your congregation. The receptionist said, "Ms. you need to talk with my pastor's wife, she is a breast cancer survivor." I shouted in my mind, Amen! Amen! Hallelujah, glory to the Most High. She gave me the pastor's wife's number, and the rest was history. Looking forward to giving the seminar! Amen! Glory!

I called another church only to find out that the pastor had experienced it personally and had a member on the church going through it at this same moment. He said, they called the Cancer Society in Jamaica, and they did not have anyone to send in that area. "Lord, here I am willing, able, and ready". 'Send me, your servant". Oh my Jesus had to die and carried all of our sins; so he can carry me. Glory to God!

This was the one that affected me most. I found an email address from a media outlet and emailed a letter asking for time on the radio station. About 1 am the next morning, my friend woke me up, because we needed the book to send to the publisher that Monday morning. I got up, went online to retrieve the book, and I saw this new e-mail. I had overlooked it, because the e-mail had a personal name and I thought it was another junk e-mail. After reading the book and cutting and pasting the text I needed, I was about to log off when I took another look at the email and decided to open it. I would like to let you know that sometimes we have doubts about doing something; just pray and ask God for the discernment to know when he is giving the green light to go ahead.

After reading the e-mail, I wanted to scream out, but my husband was sleeping right beside me in the bed and I did not want to awaken him. One of the media respondents said my story was inspiring and that he wished to connect me with his breast cancer listeners. Now tell me that the Holy Spirit is not working. Within two weeks of getting the book to the publisher, I was given the green light again by God. "Lord, I got it, I got it. Lord, if I had sat home complaining and feeling sorry for myself, I would not have seen that this was a blessing for me and most of all, the blessing that I will be for many people ahead of me.

Please allow me to say, in spite of and despite my trials, my weakness, and my health issues, I am content with me. I thank you Lord for bringing me this far. Thank you for allowing me to touch the dirtiest part of your robe, the hem. Through touching the hem of your garment, I am made new with a mission and a ministry to tell the world. You are magnificent, you are able, and all the praises belong to you.

Satan, I will say again, "you would like to let me think that my past issue is still ongoing, but I am here to let you know that I have found a new life. Please do not knock on my door anymore. You are history and you are a liar."

Nobody can take me back to where I was. My past is my blessing for me today! As for me, if anyone asks you what's the matter with Yvonne, tell them I am saved, sanctified, and baptized. I am running for my life. Who wants to be consumed by such hatred, which is like a tornado inside them? Not me. As someone rightly said, "to hold a grudge is like drinking poison and expecting the other person to die." Wherever you are, please enjoy a big laugh. I am giving you permission.

I once heard a pastor, who said the most disturbing part about holding a grudge is that the other person may have moved on and made peace with God, while you are there running up your blood pressure and having a heart attack. For me, the ongoing stress over the years allowed all kinds of ailments in my body. It only hurts you, and who knows that more than I, the perfect example. Life is too short! I choose to love, because it is less weighty than hating someone. I am free from my past, happy to know that a storm can happen around me and I will not be touched or affected by it.

Lord, keep my mind and soul upon you at all times. A friend of mine, who lives in Florida, sent me a message on Facebook. His exact words were, "Girl you are making yourself so busy doing God's work, not even Satan can catch up with you."

I replied, "Amen to that!"

I found a new purpose on which to concentrate my energy: Breast Cancer Awareness and I love it. Can you imagine that I am retiring with a great job, Breast Cancer ministry? When the book is finished, I am looking forward to writing my second. My God, my husband, and I have partnered to spread His gospel. He has work for me to do. Do you realize how many souls can be won when Jesus and I work together? Lord had you not allowed me to have breast cancer; I might have ended up losing my soul.

2 Chronicles 7: 14: My God says, *"if only my people would humble themselves, pray, call upon my name and turn from their wicked ways"*. *"Then, only then, he will forgive us and heal us"*.

"Oh! What a promise! Lord I am asking you to keep me humble, use me, and allow my life to become a beacon. I give you all". I am standing on the promises of God, and then I cannot fall. I am not twenty-one, so I will not spend time wondering why people act the way they do. I do not care to fight any battle any longer. Whenever I see Satan coming towards me with his fist clenched, I will run to Christ.

Matthew 11: 28: My God said, *"Come all who are weary and burdened down and he will give us rest"*. He said the peace that he gives is not of this miserable world. Those are the promises I stand on. Amen!

Where do I see myself within the next five years? What are my short-term goals?
First, I must say the doctors said statistically they are giving me five to ten years. My God said that he is giving me until he, God, is finished with me on earth. Let's get that out of the way. The year 2012 will be a trial and error year for me. I am putting my all and all into the ministry. I will be in Jamaica for January to the end of March 2013. I also have London, Belize, and St. Croix on my list for 2013. All work with no fun makes Jack a dull boy; so I am designing the London trip around my birthday. I am also planning a trip to Africa, which is on my bucket list. I would love to see Nelson Mandela before he dies. I have suffered on earth too much, not to see my Jesus. Now, this is not hard, because I am willing to let him use me around the four corners of the

world to finish his work. I have the best job ever. I am getting to see the world while I spread the good news of Jesus' saving grace.

If you had asked me this question a couple of years ago, my answer would have been, to go to church and get as much wealth as possible. Satan peered into my future and saw what God had in store for me and that is why he tried to kill me. My God has a job here for me to do.

I am ecstatic about my job and I take it very seriously. This is why I told Satan's agents to get out of my way, in the name of the Lord!

My greatest wish and heart's desire is to see every one of us sitting at Jesus' feet. In that way, I don't have to ask where is Ms. C, or where is Mr. C. I smile and laugh because I choose to do so; it diminishes my trials. My trials are opportunities for God to build me up and display me as an inspiration and a guiding light. I now see trials as tests. The main thing I have learned is that I must not ruffle my feathers when they come.

My God knew about them before they even attacked me, and so he already has the means to resolve them. Why worry when I can pray?

My wish and my actions are to allow God to make me into a person who will not tear anyone down ever again, but who rather builds up the weak links. I want to help lift, encourage, and motivate; not to discourage anyone, but to cool the flames of discord and not add fuel to the fire.

Breast Cancer Awareness Foundation

Being a breast cancer survivor gives one a fresh perspective on life. I have come to recognize what my true role in life is today. I need to spread the good news of Christ's love for mankind. He does not want us to die. His wish for us is for a long, healthy life.

3 John: 1-2 says, *"Beloved, I wish above all things that thou mayest prosper and be in health, even as thy soul prospereth"*.

I wish to tell everyone about my experience and let them realize the importance of getting tested for this dreadful disease, and of keeping your hope and self-confidence up. Recognize that God wants you to live, not just survive.

I hope I have been able to illustrate that theme throughout my book. As a follow-up to writing the book, I want to do public speaking. I want to start a foundation, whose aims are:

1. Help women who are undergoing chemotherapy and have no one to help at home.
2. My group must be able to send a member to go to that woman's home and sit with her and help her around the home, while she is recuperating.
3. To be able to assist a friend in making the horrible decision to take off one or two breasts or to encourage a woman to do reconstructive surgery.

We know that just like any other business, we will need financial support to start, but my Father is rich in resources. If He calls me to start, He will finish the rest. My job is to step out in faith. If anyone reading this book would like to be a part of this organization, whether by volunteering or through a donation, please contact me. The name of the organization is feed the Fight- Breast Cancer Awareness. Website www. Letsfightbreastcancer.org

I want the organization to be able to assist in providing mammogram screenings, wigs for chemo patients, sleeves for lymphedema, gloves for patients, and special fitted bras. This may sound trivial to a regular person, but they are extremely necessary for boosting one's self-esteem again. It is my dream and aspiration to be able to help in this manner. I believe it to be my true calling. I have already visited Europe and Antigua on my Breast Cancer Awareness trips. I hope to continue doing so, until I have spanned the globe with my message of hope for women.

CHAPTER 10

Trust in God

Words can cut into ones heart and allow one to be dysfunctional and crippled.

We may never understand God's wisdom. We just have to trust Him. Your trials may not be wrapped like mine, but all of us have to carry our own cross, just like Jesus. Whatever is going on in your life today, if you think you cannot go on anymore, please turn it over to Jesus. Your mountain is not as big as you think. Sometimes God has already cut out some steps to allow you to track your way up to the top of the mountain. He is waiting for that call. He even takes collect calls, texts, emails, and tweets. Whatever means of communication you want, He is ready and waiting. Whenever you call you will not hear, *"Please leave a message and I will get right back to you."* He is the receptionist. He will answer you right away. God is good all the time, through good and bad times.

Matthew 6:28-29 says, *"Consider the lilies of the field and how they grow; they toil not, neither do they spin; And yet I say unto you, that even Solomon in all his glory was not arrayed like one of these."*

Trust in the Lord with all your heart, He will provide for you, and will take care of you. After all He's your dad. If God allows things to happen to you, it is because He already provided all the apparatus for you.

Recognition

I am truly blessed in every sense of the word. Throughout my ordeals I was able to keep my smile and find my inner peace. I am right here to stay with my family. What God blesses must stay blessed. *"Step out of our way Satan! The God of the mountain is also the God of the valley. Thank you Jesus!"*

When God puts His hand on our problems, the problems become insignificant. This does not mean Satan has stopped looking for opportunities to put his foot in. *"Lord, thank you for the valley, because it helps us appreciate the mountain."* We had to wipe many tears from our eyes, but we are still holding each other's hands. God has proven His love to me so many times. He has truly brought me through the storms. I hope this book will inspire, uplift and encourage the young and the old to hold on and not give up. Brighter days are coming as long as you trust in God.

I have learned that happiness and joy do not necessarily mean Satan is sleeping. As my storm raged, I still found the inner peace that passes all understanding. At the end of the day, I will continue to let Satan know that he is a liar. I have grown in Christ.

During treatment, my husband supported and cared for me immensely. I can remember my husband holding my hands letting me know he would be there for me and that God would not give us more than we could bear. For a long time, the devil was trying to break us up, but he is a liar. No height, no depth, not even the ravages of stage 3 cancer could put a wedge between us. Instead, our love grew even stronger.

"My children, my children, Oh God, thank you for them! "

Yvonna, my baby, has been a source of such support. What I remember most about Yvonna is that when I came home from the hospital after my surgery with tubes projecting all over, Yvonna would give me daily baths with love and tender care. She would gently make sure that the bandages did not get wet and the tubes remained in place.

Coleen, the dainty one, my precious made sure I got everything that I needed. I remember Coleen sleeping with me on the nights after my surgeries.

Chadeesia, my beloved nurse, was there at each surgery. She would go to work the night following each surgery, but come to the hospital in the mornings to clean me up. Also, I want to use this time to apologize to Chadeesia, I was so mentally worn out because of what I was going through over the years and not wanting to see any of you guys fail in life, that my parenting skills took on another level of discipline. Now, I recognized that I was too, too harsh on you. I am extremely proud of your accomplishments, and most of all I love you so much. I truly give God thanks for carrying me over those struggling years.

Tanya, my sweet daughter, my nurse, relocated from Florida just to take care of me. Every time she took me to the doctor, she would have her little piece of paper with a hundred questions to ask the doctor. She is such a sweet soul. You have integrated in our family so well and I love you more than mangoes (smile) for that I give God all the praise.

My support was intact because they were sent from heaven. Marcus Huggan was my special supporter who insisted I play a game of dominoes the day after I came home from the hospital, so I would forget about my pain; and to this day we still play dominoes. He spent the entire summer cheering me up and insisted I attend his

High School graduation even with the tubes sticking out of my body!

From the guys who played dominoes with me every night except on the Sabbath (Jean & Lloyd Hamilton, Steve, Paul, Lassalle, Clifford, Marcus, King, and Gordene), Pastor Daley and his wife, Lorna Fraser, and Carolyn Blake; I had all the support I needed.

I am grateful for the Golden Girls of Lithonia SDA church. Mrs. Shaw who insisted on being by my bedside when I awoke from surgeries, Mrs. Hazel who was at every visit I had at the doctors, Mrs. Boswell the counselor, when I needed emergency surgeries to repair my chemo port. While I was sitting in the room waiting for the nurse to take me to the OR, Mrs. Boswell was counseling me about maintaining a healthy love life. She said that many marriages break apart, because the wife becomes so absorbed in the illness that she forgets to spend time with her husbands. I am also thankful for the members of Central Islip SDA Church, who prayed as a body for me. I am thankful for my Emmanuel SDA church family, and the Hudson family for all those prayers. The blessings did come down.

I am thankful for my cousin Beverly Salmon's (who lives in St. Ann, Jamaica) early morning bible studies and sing-a-longs. When I was first diagnosed, I could not sleep and our talks and songs at 2 am in the morning helped me through these tough times. I thank my young people from church; my weekly Sabbath morning calls from Sally Ann, Natalie Smith from Negril, Wilfred Beckford, otherwise known as Bousie, Anthony Trott; Kenya Brown, who took time off from her job in Jamaica to keep me company; my sister Angella, who has been my nurse and doctor. I thank my brother Peter and his family who were here the moment they heard. I also thank my numerous friends and family from Facebook and the Sinclair family and my husband's family. There were so many people who walked with me through my breast cancer journey I just want to say thank you all. I am so grateful for the many godly people who prayed for me. I attribute my speedy recovery to all of their support and the love I felt.

God has reassured me that He is my refuge and strength, a very present help in trouble.

Ps. 46:1 says, *"Therefore I will not fear, though the earth gives way and though the mountains crumble around us"*.

As long as I abide in Him, I am okay. We thank you, Lord, for walking with us on our journey. Most of all I want to let the world know that wherever the Lord allows you to be, stay there and be content. I will use my lemons to make lemonade and be a resource to someone who was just diagnosed with cancer. "What a refreshing drink in the summer!"

Making a difference

Today we are in year 2012, and as a forty-eight year old woman reflecting on my life, if I could go back to school I would major in psychology. Now, I see how broadly culture impacts us, the community, the family, and the individual. Even though we may live in the same country and the same district and even attend the same church, we still have our own individual beliefs.

Every family has its own culture! Each family is unique in its own ways. The way a family makes decisions, how the world is perceived, the belief system, habits are all different for each and every family. Some families are tightly tied to their norms and habits regardless of whether these traditions are healthy or unhealthy.

Today, I can say that I literally live my life as the words of that song I sang thirty years ago at my high school graduation – "No Man is an Island". Call me naïve but my door is always open to everyone. You can come to my home knowing that before you leave you will have a hot meal or something to eat. I remember being laughed at by my extended family for cooking so much food (in a good way). I do not own a small pot. Mine are the size of pots used in restaurants. I took it a little further to make sure this was instilled in my children.

Why did I do that? Because I wanted my children to realize the needs of those around them, to look out for others and to know that the world does not start or finish with them. I now understand why God instructs us.

Proverbs 22:6 says to *"train up a child the way he should grow, because when they are old they will not depart from it."*

I am in no way trying to be self-righteous; to the contrary. As parents who believe in Christ, it is important to be careful what we impart to our children. We need to remember to take them out of the self-center bubble, teach them to reach out to others, and help them to think of others as they think of themselves.

1 Peter 1:22 says: *"Having purified your souls by your obedience to the truth for a sincere brotherly love, love one another earnestly from a pure heart."*

1 John 4:7 *"Beloved, let us love one another, for love is from God, and whoever loves has been born of God and knows God."*

John 15:12-15 *"This is my commandment, that you love one another as I have loved you. Greater love has no one than this that someone lay down his life for his friends. You are my friends if you do what I command you. No longer do I call you servants, for the servant does not know what his master is doing; but I have called you friends, for all that I have heard from my Father I have made known to you".*

Phil. 2:1-4 says, *"Therefore if there is any consolation in Christ, if any comfort of love, if any fellowship (communion) of the Spirit, if any affection and mercy, fulfill my joy by being like-minded, having the same love, being of one accord, of one mind. Let nothing be done through selfish ambition or conceit, but in lowliness of mind let each esteem others better than himself. Let each of you look out not only for your interests, but also for the interests of others."*

I believe that in order for one to follow the instructions given in the verse I mentioned, you have to have a personal relationship with Christ. The love of Christ has to be in you. You have to know and be comfortable with yourself, know who you are, who you put your trust in before you can elevate others. And you can only do that by knowing God. The God whom I have come to know even more today says He is LOVE.

Phil. 2:5-11 says, *"Let this mind be in you which was also in Christ Jesus, who, being in the form of God, did not consider it robbery to be equal with God, but made Himself of no reputation, taking the form of a bond-servant and coming in the likeness of men. And being found in appearance as a man, He humbled himself and became obedient to point of death, even death of the cross. Therefore God also has exalted Him and given the name which is above every Name, that at the Name of Jesus every knee should bow, of those in Heaven, and of those on earth, and those under the earth, and that every tongue should confess that Jesus Christ is Lord, to Glory of God the Father".*

Oh the blessings that await us by living close to God. Let us consciously put these wonderful words of God in practice. God would not tell us to do something if he did not think we could do it.

Life will always have storms in it, but it is our choice whether we let it drown us or whether we hold on to God's word instead. In my past, I wondered, deliberated and pondered too long over people's behavior toward my children. I took life too seriously. I did that because of my upbringing. I thought the world should be a good and safe place to encourage, reassure, inspire and support one another. I believe that if my neighbor's child fails, then my child fails, also. I have now come to realize that not everyone thinks like that and I should not be resentful or force my values onto anyone, because they don't share my beliefs.

I saw the world as an ideal place when I was a teenager. Now I see a "dog-eat-dog" world, where it is everyone for themselves and God for us all. A friend of mine said to me just a week ago, that it was because of my personality that God chose me to bring this ministry of breast cancer awareness to the four corners of the world. She said, frankly, if she had been chosen, she would have curled up in her bed and felt sorry for herself and thought the world had done her wrong. So she is thankful that people like me go out and encourage others, to avoid the ordeal of breast cancer and protect the children.

While I may have no control over my worries, I do have control over my actions; and on this note, I choose to be better, not bitter in life.

In conclusion, I would like to remind everyone that life's journey is not a bed of roses and that is the reason God made provision for man to come back to him. Life is made up of choices. We have to choose, either the wide road that leads to hell, where everyone does what they feel is right (It is the road that is paved with good intentions, where you will see well-schooled people, and the stubborn ones who are proud to say they are too old to change their destructive ways that batter and damage others); or, we can choose the narrow road that leads to heaven. Here our task is to humble ourselves, trust God in all parts of our lives, and make God our center. My wish is that this book will help you whenever you reach a crossroad in life and you don't know where to turn, because you are disheartened, distressed and worried. That you will find some hope, something to hold on to, but most of all, that you will look to Christ.

For the children, my heart and home are readily open to you. What I see now destroying young people around me are parents who are not doing their heavenly duties. The choice of standing up for children was not hard; and if I had to do it again, I would do it in a heartbeat, even though it took a toll on my body. Every day, I pray the Lord will surround every child on this earth, especially those who are hurting. I believe that if we don't like something, instead of nurturing the pain, cuddling the hurt, and covering up the mess, we can become an advocate.

I choose to smile! That does not mean I am not in pain. It means I am putting my life into perspective. I have learned a valuable lesson. I have been given another lease on life. I am a wounded person trying to make heaven my home. I cannot erase the past and I cannot wipe out the adversity I experienced, but I can smile my way through the future and watch how God unfolds and takes me to higher ground. Statistically, I am given five to ten years to live. I am accepting it and I will run with it, glorify God with it, spread breast cancer awareness with it, and love my family, my extended family, my friends and the universe. I have found my divine calling and I am answering it. *"Use me Lord!"*

If I had not been tested, I would not able to share my testimony today. If God had not helped me with my mess, I would not have a message to share. I am using my adversity to advertise that I serve a risen Savior. I am just a survivor of Cancer standing on God's promises.

My Father was able to carry me safely through my storm. I am not the same physically. I have lots of medical issues, but I don't have to worry about anything, because I am also not the same spiritually. One day, yes! One day, when the earth is made new, I will be covered in white robes and made in his image again. I am looking forward to the place where there is no pain, no tears, no sickness, but only laughter, smiles, and mangoes to eat.(smile)

See you there!

Laughter the Best Medicine

I happen to be blessed. My blessings outweigh my trials. I had the greatest husband in my corner and children who helped me every step of the way. I also had a group of friends who traveled with me to Jamaica a year after my mastectomy. One day one of the ladies who was very funny looked at me with a dead-pan face and said, "Yvonne, every morning you wake up with a different color breast."

As I had not done my reconstruction, anything I could find to fill up my bra I would use. Sometimes I would use a sock, a t-shirt, as long as it had bulk to give me the semblance of a breast and I would stick it in my bra. The point is that your mental outlook is what matters when fighting such devastation. I could easily have stayed home and hosted my own pity party, but I was determined to live and not die. I chose not to let the world go on without me having a place in it. Most of all, I lived to accomplish my true purpose of being on this earth.

There is a saying in the book of Proverbs that gives us the key to bearing all illnesses. It says, "A merry heart doeth good like medicine!" If I had my life to live over again, I would not change any part of it. God gave me a gem for a husband. I would not trade him in for the world. We both grew in all aspect of our life. And the good thing is that we grew together which made us more in love with each other.

You kept my family sane through it all! Thank you!

Testimonials from Friends and Family

It is amazing how our choices can empower and impact others, even without our consciously knowing it! At the age of ten, I was given a Bible text to memorize at the Glendevon Seventh-day Adventist Church in Montego Bay, St. James:

"In the same way, let your light shine before others, so that they may see your good works and give glory to your Father who is in heaven" (Matt: 5-16)

Little did I know it would impact my life for the next thirty-eight years? I am not claiming to be perfect at all, and I have many bad days; but through the grace and mercy of God in my life every day, I can truly claim that God is good to me.

Colin

Upon getting the bad news of breast cancer, the entire family was saddened and devastated. However, this sadness could only spend a few days in the house with Yvonne. After a few days, she accepted her condition and decided that nothing was going to take her smile away. Often when friends would come to visit her they were amazed to see how upbeat she was. They would leave feeling as if they were the ones that were sick. I think it was the positive way of dealing with the sickness and the strong family support that caused her to overcome cancer; and this attitude will take her through the rest of her life. Let me say that for me, I would not even think of writing a book, because I am an extremely private man. On the other hand, I married a high spirited, daring, bold, zealous, and passionate woman. Over the years and even more now, I have come to admire and appreciate her for using her adversities and misfortunes for the betterment of society. Those who know her will attest that she does not do anything on a small scale. So, I am joining her hands and heart to go global with her ministries. I am so proud of my wife's strength and fortitude. Yvonne, I support and love you. Colin Dunkley, your husband.

Natalie

Ever since the first day I met Yvonne, she has impacted my life and continues to do so even today. The first day I met her, she invited me to her home and I felt no apprehension. Yvonne has a warm and vibrant personality that exudes whenever you interact with her, no matter her circumstances.

One of the things that fascinates me about her is her disconnect from the material world. There is nothing too great for her to give or share. She is not bound to or trapped by the inanimate. Yvonne is so full of life; she smiles easily, she talks easily and always wants the best for everyone.

I am particularly impressed with the way she handles her illness. I consider myself a realist, living by the notion of "what is to be must be." I try not to be floored by anything, but when I got that dreadful news I was floored. "Not Yvonne," I thought. "You don't take life so soon from someone like Yvonne," I argued. "She has too much to give," I fussed. I hastily ended the call, not because I had no compassion, but because I was falling apart inside and the "victim" (at the time) was positive, strong, and optimistic. I regained my composure and then I returned the call.

I have learned a valuable lesson since then, which is, what afflicts you is not the problem. The problem is how you allow it to affect you.

Since then, she has continued to inspire me and many others through Facebook. She even went to Antigua to minister about breast cancer awareness. The funniest thing about her is that she is not even well physically. One of her medical challenges is delayed memory. One would think people with PhDs, the well-schooled, and the rich should be doing this kind of ministry, but she works within her limitations, sincerely wanting to help others. This is teaching me that God can use anyone as long as we humble ourselves before him. This is the person that I am truly striving to be every day; knowing this is what God wants of me. You have touched many lives and I am one of them. Shine on Yvonne! Your flame will burn brightly in the hearts of those lives you have so generously touched for many years to come. —Natalie Smith, retired school teacher

Chadeesia

As a nurse, when I hear the word cancer, as pessimistic as it may seem, the first word that comes to mind is death. When I heard the words mammogram, breast cancer, Stage 3, all I could think was, my mom's going to die. Through the course of her sickness and treatments I have gained a new perspective for the word cancer. When I hear the word cancer, I now think of hope, miracles, tribulations and trials, family, and faith; and that all things are possible with Christ. Continue to illuminate mom, you are the best! -Chadeesia Dunkley (daughter/Registered Nurse)

Tanya

I remember going to the oncologist with mom to find out her test results. Mom undressed, put her gown on and sat on the examination table as we waited for the doctor to come in. My sisters and I laughed and talked. Little did we know that our lives were going to be changed! The doctor entered the room and got quickly to the point. She told mom that she had breast cancer. I thought, "What? No, this cannot be happening, at least not to us." It seemed surreal. We all embraced mom and cried, and cried. I wondered "what happens now?" We went home and of course mom was very sad and broken up by the news. Throughout the next months of treatment mom trusted in God and His healing power. She always verbalized her faith saying that "God will bring me through." I admired her faith in God and how well she coped with her illness. Our family pulled together and supported mom during her mastectomy, chemotherapy, radiation, breast reconstruction, and medical appointments. We also had the support of close family friends who played a priceless role in mom's recovery.

I am very proud of mom. She has such a vivacious and resilient spirit. I admire how she has always managed to see the positive and God's blessing through it all. In the essence of her mantra, "better, not bitter," she was inspired to use her story to encourage and empower others. She started at local churches and then God opened the way for her to go overseas to Antigua. I know she inspired many who heard her story over the radio or at churches. I know God will continue to bless her and open up new opportunities for ministry.

For my thirtieth birthday, I wanted to go to Europe and I shared this trip with mom. We had such a wonderful time together. This trip would not have been the same without her. My wish for you mom is that you will continue to be healthy and happy. Keep laughing and living. May God continue to bless you in your ministry, I love you. — Tanya Dunkley (daughter/Registered Nurse)

Peter

It is with a sense of wonder, and sheer admiration, that one can't help but be awed by Yvonne's positive attitude that transcends even the loss of any vestige of womanhood at a seemingly dark personal hour. Just before the mastectomy, I expressed my sorrow at what I deemed to be a significant loss for any woman. Her instant response was, "sorry for what?" Being able to see her refusing to surrender her zest for life bares the bedrock of her enduring human spirit.—Peter Codrington

Elvis

At first I was shocked and then puzzled, even hurt when I was informed that you had breast cancer. After high school we lost touch with each other, then this news? We talked and I was blown away, because you did not feel sorry for yourself. You were the most positive and uplifting person I had talked with in my life. I was inspired by your approach to breast cancer. I continue to admire your uplifting attitude and positive take on life. Because of knowing you, I believe I can accept, live, and fight whatever life throws at me. I know you have bad days, but one can never get that feeling from talking to you. I am honored to be called your friend. — Elvis Sharpe

Carolyn

My name is Carolyn, and I am a breast cancer survivor of three years. Even though we lived in the same city in Jamaica and went to the same high school and

I knew her brother, who, by the way was my brother's very good friend; I did not meet Yvonne until we were both diagnosed with breast cancer. We met through Facebook. When I was first told I had breast cancer, I was in shock and total disbelief. I thought breast cancer was a disease that would never touch me. Even when I worked with other women who were survivors, in my mind, it was someone else's disease, not mine. I was feeling sorry for myself, but talking to Yvonne made me put things into perspective. Her faith and trust in the Lord was remarkable. She never wavered. She always had a smile on her face no matter what she was going through. She remained positive. When I got her call telling me she was going to Antigua and Jamaica to spread breast cancer awareness, I was so happy for her, since I knew she got the calling from God to go out and educate other women about the importance of early detection and treatment in saving their lives. Her trip to Europe for her birthday could not have happened to a better person. Spending time with family and friends and doing God's work is so important, as tomorrow is not promised to us. My wish for her is a future of blessings, love, joy, peace, and happiness and to continue the great job she is doing by spreading the awareness of breast cancer.—Carolyn Morris

Kammara

I became an elementary school teacher in Jamaica with the help of my Aunt. When I think of Yvonne Headley-Dunkley, I think of an angel! My aunt is a very caring, happy, and selfless lady. There is nothing too great for Auntie to do for anyone, be it relative or friend, or just somebody that she hears about who needs a helping hand. When I discovered that my aunt had breast cancer, I never doubted in her recovery. Auntie puts God at the center of whatever she does. God is always in control. Thus, I knew God would bring her through and she would emerge victorious. Auntie never let breast cancer get the better of her. She got the better of it. She has been an inspiration to me. She has demonstrated to me and the many lives she has touched that no matter what may come our way, God is in control and he will take care of us! I'm proud to say Yvonne Headley-Dunkley is my aunt. —Kammara Deslandes, School Teacher

Shanticka

I am truly inspired by Mrs. D, because of her will to live as well as her desire to encourage others to live life to the fullest. I worked with Mrs. D for approximately three years and during this time she was one of the best foster parents I encountered....always looking out for the best interest of the child. Mrs. D was diagnosed with breast cancer, went through chemo and radiation and all the while continuing to foster with a smile. She never once exhibited bitterness for the cards that had been dealt. A very loving and caring person that I am truly blessed to have met. Because of her, I have decided that I will forever bring awareness to Breast Cancer. This year my 12 year old daughter and I decided to wear pink every day during the month of October....small gesture I know; but big when that was just not a part of your norm. I learned to not allow the cares of the world to burden you down, but to continue to endure, because the reward God has in store is much more than any person could give. Shanticka Molly, Social Worker)

Carol

"With Jesus in the vessel we can smile at the storm as we go sailing through."

In the summer of 1982, I was walking through the lobby area of our dormitory at the West Indies College (Now Northern Caribbean University) when I was greeted by a young lady who was coming down the stairs. She had a very contagious smile as she said, "Hi, I am Yvonne Headley." That marked the beginning of a friendship that spans over thirty years.

What strikes me most about Yvonne is her ability to smile or laugh her way through any adversity. You see, she has always had Christ in her vessel.

A few years ago when Yvonne told me she was diagnosed with breast cancer, I was in shock and feared for her life, but then came that smile along with a faith that could move mountains. All through her illness, Yvonne has been an inspiration to many, including another friend, Betsy, who was, also, battling cancer. Yvonne's faith and courage and her ability to smile and laugh through her difficult situation gave Betsy much hope. Although Betsy is no longer with us, one of the last things she said to me was how blessed she was to have made the connection with Yvonne, the girl who is always smiling or laughing.

I pray that God will continue to shine his mercy on my dear friend, Yvonne Headley Dunkley. — Carol Duhaney-King

Debbie Neil

A black, strong woman! I knew Yvonne Dunkley through her husband Colin Dunkley on Facebook. Her status was always inspiring me. She is someone who loves and appreciates life and is full of life. We became friends on Facebook. I met her on her tour to Europe, and I was able to see her in the flesh. She is a person, who has grown mentally, past her physical challenges. Her Facebook status is always displaying someone who has faced trials and does not want to wear her problems on her sleeve but rather overcome adversity. Going through her breast cancer treatment, she was always happy, even when in pain. She is a breath of fresh air. While she was on her European tour, she visited us and I had to do surgery. She postponed going home and meeting her longtime school friends she had not seen for over twenty years. She stayed at the hospital during my surgery and was one of the persons there when I awoke from the anesthesia. My aunt said she just had to come to the house to meet her to see if she was just as full of life in the flesh, because she had seen her on Facebook and she was just so inspirational and lively.— Debbie Oneil (U.K.)

Dawn

It is very interesting how we lose track of some friends and then God allows them to reappear in your life at a very special time. I followed Yvonne's journey on Facebook as she cheerfully fought breast cancer. Her journey was one of praise and empowerment. If a person could be cheerful and strong while fighting an illness, this was definitely the person. She travelled and celebrated her journey when time allowed .She was also willing to open her doors and heart to loving others and to be a great hostess. ~juju

Dawn

I first met Yvonne in Montego Bay, Jamaica, in 1981. I was the Accountant for the Harrison Memorial High School, where she attended. She was a bright, bubbly, effervescent, and always laughing student. Yvonne was not only a pleasant, energetic person, but someone who behaved quite maturely for her age. She had not only the respect of the staff at the school, but even more so that of her peers and the younger students. She was one of those students who looked forward for lunch time to play netball. She always looked out for the concerns and well-being of others.

When I heard that Yvonne was diagnosed with breast cancer, although I was shocked and disappointed with the diagnosis, she never brought depression, despair, or anger into her life when talking to me about it. She motivated and inspired so many of us with her positive attitude, and her ability to live her life as if nothing had changed. I see the spirit of God in Yvonne, so large that it even encompasses me and all her family and friends. Yvonne is definitely a person whom I will never forget. She used her laughter to take herself out of distress. I know that all is well in her heart because she shares breast cancer awareness with others and gives testimony to the goodness of Christ. My prayers are with her and her family always. I shall always remember this awesome young lady who, when adversity touched her, stood strong like a brave. May God continue to bless her and the ministry as she tours the Caribbean countries telling people how early testing and treatment saves lives! Blessings always Yvonne!

—Dawn Daley (Orlando, Florida)

Petrona

The first time I met Yvonne, I was immediately drawn to her, due to her warmth, kindness, and pleasant personality. Yvonne is always laughing, and nothing seems to bother her. The thing I admire most is her relationship with her four daughters, and how she brought them up to be successful young ladies. Yvonne's house is never out of food. She loves to feed people, and there is never a time when I enter her house and leave hungry. I remember vividly the day when I had the nagging feeling to call Yvonne. I picked up my cell phone and dialed her number, and when she answered the phone she asked me if I had heard. I said, "Heard what?" and then she told me that she was diagnosed with breast cancer. At that very moment, my body felt numb and I could feel a shiver going through me and I started to cry. During my sobbing I could hear Yvonne laughing. At first I didn't understand what was going on. I said to her, "I am crying, why are you laughing?" She said, "Don't cry, because God would not allow me to have breast cancer if he was not going to be there for me." With a happy voice, she said, "God has come through for me before, He and I will handle breast cancer. I will never ask God, "Why me?" I will only ask," Why not me?" After hearing these words I was able to calm down. We spoke for an hour then hung up.

After hanging up with Yvonne, I called my fiancé Stewart, who is a childhood friend of Yvonne's husband, Colin. During my conversation with him, trying to explain Yvonne's plight, I could not help it, but I broke down and cried. As a nurse I knew the treatment she had to face was going to be rigorous on her body, rough mentally, and just a rocky road. Also I knew the doctors had to explain the brutal, vicious, and harsh details about the treatment and what was to be expected, but this did not break Yvonne's spirit. Her strength, courage, and most importantly her love for God has brought her through one of the darkest moments of her life. Yvonne is truly a remarkable being who God placed on earth. There is no doubt in my mind that she will continue to fight. — Petrona Henry, Nurse

Cimone

I have known Yvonne for many years. I knew her in high school, but we became friends as adults. I was in Jamaica when I heard the news of her being diagnosed with breast cancer. I was saddened to hear of the dreadful diagnosis and the only thought I had was, "Please God, do not allow it to break her spirit." She is such a happy, joyous soul that it would be a loss to humankind to lose such a happy spirit.

I was more than happy to help. I took pleasure in hearing her story. She has gone through a lot, but her faith and laughter have taken her through the rain. Her family and friends have been supportive and her response to a second lease on life is wonderful to behold. She makes every day count and she constantly gives God the praise. Breast cancer is only a disease. I am happy she has been smiling through it all and I know she will take this message of breast cancer awareness to one and all. She wants to offer real hope to others by letting them know that this is not a death sentence, but a chance for renewal of their life.—Cimone Brown

Shirolene Bingham Armstrong

As a facilitator of a prominent university in Montego Bay, Jamaica, I was leading a devotional session before facilitating the lesson for the evening. The theme for discussion had to do with being thankful and students were making their contribution toward the theme.

One student reflected on a day when she visited a friend's home and was amazed at the fact that one of her friend's family members, who is a cancer survivor, was so optimistic and was just celebrating life. The discussion ensued for a while about this person's positive approach to life despite her challenges and the obvious level of thankfulness and praise to God for blessing her with life.

We reflected on the goodness of God and the many blessings He has bestowed on us all; yet we complain, we worry and we are unthankful at times when some very small material aspect is out of place in our lives. At a point in the discussion, the student mentioned that I should know the person we were speaking about, but for some reason, the name was not familiar at that time (I did not know her married name).

Devotion ended and we had a very interactive class on Human Resource Management that evening. When I reached home that evening, very uncommon to my routine, I went on Facebook and as many of us do 'I checked out what everybody was discussing'. It was then I saw a profile photo of a female who seemed to be having the time of her life. To my amazement, she went by the same name my student had mentioned earlier in class, Yvonne Dunkley. Upon close investigation, I realized she was my long lost schoolmate and neighbor. I perused her photos in awe as I pondered the question, "How can one who has experienced such a challenge be living such a life of praise and thanksgiving?"

My only conclusion is that once you have a relationship with Jesus, He gives you joy everlasting and peace beyond understanding. Yvonne, the fact that your experience reflected in true thankfulness and praise to God is an indication that you are touching the lives of many as a result of your relationship with Him. Continue to be an instrument in His hands to bless others.

- Shirolene Bingham Armstrong

Caroline Smith

Caroline was another friend I grew up with. She told me about her mother, whom I would say was in her seventies. Her mom is sickly and she had to give her medicine to her before she goes to school (she also is a teacher). She said her mother always gave her a hard time when taking her medicine. One night when she read my Facebook status, she could feel the pain I was in, but I was still giving God the praise. She said that morning she used my experience to show her mother that there are people worse off than she was and encouraged her to look at my circumstances. She told her, "Polly is sicker than you, Mother." She said that after telling her mom what was going on with me, her mother gave God thanks and took her medicine. "To God be the glory!" Yvonne Headley Dunkley

Doreen

Here is a quote from the Clear Word Bible Ps. 78:4-8: "We will not hide from our children the things which we have received, but will tell the next generation about the Lord's glorious power, His great deeds, and the wonderful things He has done. He wrote out His laws for His people Israel and gave His commandments to the descendants of Jacob; He told our fathers to pass them on to their children. This way the next generation can know them and in turn, pass them on to their children. So all generations will learn to put their trust in God and not forget what He has done."

We must be careful what legacy we are leaving with our children, because God is going to hold us responsible if, due to our selfishness, we make choices which cause the next generation to lose their way. Whether we believe it or not, our choices today will impact future generations. Personally I would not want my choices to cause the next generation to neglect God's law and miss out on so great a salvation.

Yvonne, my dear friend and sister, I can truly say that during the time of your illness you did not change or lose your cheerful self, nor did I detect any wavering of your faith, even though you were in pain. Instead, you were more inspiring and encouraging than ever. You were the "sick" one, yet you were able to lift my spirits while I was going through difficult times in my life. My brother, the pastor, is thrilled to have you at his church on your breast cancer awareness tour in Jamaica, 2013.

Yvonne you are a true reflection of the SON in my eyes, keep shining! I love you my sister. Doreen Dennis, Accountant

Lorna James

I think the best testimony was from a friend who came to look for me one Sabbath. When she came in the house, she told me she wanted to come for a long time, but she was afraid, contemplating what to say to a friend who is diagnosed with a death sentence. So, she had to build up the courage. To her surprise, when I greeted her at the door, all her sadness disappeared to the point where she was wondering, which one of us was sick. She said the moment I opened the door, with that wide contagious smile, she instantly felt great. She said she was surprised, because I was as happy as a clown. We spoke for about two hours and at the end of the visit she said to me, "Yvonne, I am inspired by your life." She went on to say, "That she is a nurse and on Zoloft". She said, "She did not get a death sentence and if anyone had, it was me; and yet I was as chirpy as a bird". A day or two later, she called me to let me know, She took herself off Zoloft, the anti-depressant. She said, I could not comprehend what this visit had done for her. She is making big changes in her life, because she did not get a death sentence; as far as she knows, you did!

To God is the glory!

By Yvonne Headley Dunkley

Mrs. Eucene Hazel

I met one of my "mothers", Mrs. Eucene Hazel, when she left Boston and came to live in Atlanta, where I sold her a house, and we grew close.

When she heard I was sick, she came that Sunday to pray with and for me. When I started chemotherapy, she would come every morning to accompany me to my appointments along with my family. She would say, "Yvonne, come sit right beside me. I will drive you." Mrs. Hazel did not miss one of my appointments and sometimes I had three appointments per week. She went even further and wrote down my appointments for me, because I had become forgetful from the chemo. One morning when she came for me, I said that I wanted to give her some gas money to help with the fuel. She said to me, "Don't you ever say a thing like that again!" In this society, we think that we can't do something good without wanting something back. I will not let anything block my blessing from God. Oh how I love her and all the rest of the Golden Girls from Lithonia Seventh-day Adventist Church. She was sent from God to lighten up my life. Her candle burned extremely bright during my illness." "To God be the glory. I will continue to hold someone else's hands, letting them know it is endurable if you allow God to captain your ship, because you Mrs. Hazel have loved me just like a child you have given birth." By Yvonne Dunkley

Coleen Dunkley

On April 22, 2010 my mother called me to let me know, she had breast Cancer. I was at my friend's home. I was numb, motionless, frightened and traumatized. I am a psychology major and it is funny how one sentence can turn one's life into chaos. I tried to compose myself, but how does one calm oneself after such bad news. My grandma and my grandpa were gone and I knew I could not and did not want to go through such emotional devastation again. My grandparents had died a year or two ago and I had not gotten over the grief. I felt as if I could not handle this. I was zoned out from the world. I was at every surgery and most of the chemo treatments, because then I was a sophomore student.

My mother is a strong, black woman! Thinking back on Maya Angelou's poem, I saw her describing my mother. A phenomenal woman! She calmed everyone's fears and asked us to stand on the promises of God knowing he will get us through. Her words are, "If God allows it; he will take care of it." She allowed her faith, her commitment and her belief to define life at that perilous time.

She continues to amaze her friends, family and I. My mom wrote a book at a time when her brain is impaired. She would take forever to write one paragraph, then another and now a book. Who does a thing like that? She plans to touch people's lives in the same way with breast cancer awareness. I have come to realize that there is nothing in this world that is impossible with God. She proudly exemplified a strength that can only come from God. I am overwhelmed and proud of her taking the message of breast cancer awareness to the world especially the under- developing countries. She used a bad situation, turned it into something positive, and for that I say, she is an example for us. "You are awesome and you have been a great mom, not just to us, but to all the children who have passed your way. Mother, continue to hold up your banner for Christ and most of all to your friends and us. Lots of blessing to you now and forever"! Coleen Dunkley daughter, BS. Psychology

Yvonna

I admire my mother's strength even when evil forces tried to convince my mother to abort me. That still voice was able to command her. The sheep heard his voice. "Thank you Jesus!" Mom, you did a great job with the little resources you had. You were able to raise four ladies and touch the lives of many young people, and now you are going global. There is no valley too deep and no ocean too wide, no mountain too high that with God and you cannot climb. Mom, I can see you sparkling from afar. Go Mother! Continue to allow God to shine within you. -- Yvonna (Daughter)

Sandra Knight

When I first heard of your cancer I was shocked, I said NO!! Not bubbly Yvonne. Remembering your own words a year before... "If I should die do not cry for me, I have lived my life to the fullest". Right there and then I remembered my resilient friend...Yvonne. This type of resilience was demonstrated in your Facebook notes and our telephone conversations. You inspired me daily, but more so when I was told I needed to do emergency surgery myself. Speaking to you that night before doing that procedure strengthened my faith in God. Your trips to both Antigua and Jamaica are a directive from God. I am praying earnestly for God to continue use you as a missionary to his daughters. – Sandra Knight, Friend

Melissa

When Yvonne was born they broke the mold as I have never met another soul quite like her. She is truly representative of what it means to be a disciple of Christ. It is 'one thing' to covet the title of "Christian" and it's 'another thing' to demonstrate Christ's attributes of character. I believe her pursuit of happiness and her drive to make all things right, as well as her immeasurable zest for life, has fueled Yvonne on her journey through Breast Cancer. She has completely surrendered her life and will to the Great Physician and has given herself wholly to His service. What greater accomplishment could one attain?

I began my reading of Yvonne's account of her ongoing battle with breast cancer and the trials that had prepared the way with much apprehension. Unsure of what I would have encountered, I began my editing. Despite the typical corrections, I found myself engrossed in a story her daughters had accurately described as riveting! As I edited, I discovered that tears were rolling down my cheeks, because her emotions had touched me on so many levels. There is a lesson for everyone! Most certainly, the writing of this book was commissioned by a 'Greater Power'!

The 'character' that stood out to me, second only to Yvonne, was Colin, her husband. Habitually, we as wives take for granted the power of God to work on the human heart, often times unseen by man and we lack the faith and longsuffering to stay the course with God! We don't believe change is likely to occur. I also applaud her daughters as their tenacity of support resonates in my own experience with my father's illness.

This real life story is fervently touching, yet funny. It will not only give you an insight into Jamaican culture and dialect, but it will dramatically transform your outlook on life – forever!

Melissa Bonnick-Anderson – Editor

Bonnick.editor@gmail.com
dwn2ert@aol.com

Feed the Fight- Breast Cancer Awareness
Visit us at http: WWW. Letsfightcancer.org

Some of the Scriptures used

James 1:3	Isa 41:10
Matt 5:19	1John 4:4
2 Timothy 1:7	1 Thessalonians 4:16-18
Matthew 17:201	Thessalonians 5:9-10

Citation
Bible

Mayo Clinic. Mayo Foundation for Medical Education and Research, n.d. Web. 23 May 2012.

"American Cancer Society | Information and Resources for Cancer: Breast, Colon, Lung, Prostate, Skin." *American Cancer Society | Information and Resources for Cancer: Breast, Colon, Lung, Prostate, Skin.* N.p., n.d. Web. 23 May 2012.

"Cancer Fighting Strategies." N.p., n.d. Web. 23 May 2012.

"Bible Gateway." *King James Version (KJV Bible).* N.p., n.d. Web. 23 May 2012.

To: Tanya, Chadeesia, Coleen, Yvonna, and all the young people out there,

I want to leave with you this mantra;

The world can be a miserable place, but for now that's what we have so make the best of it. Take pride in yourself and cherish people, because that is what God requires of you. Stop to smile the fresh flowers as they bloom, because tomorrow they will wither away. Be positive and keep God's love in your heart, because there is no other love like His. Be at peace with yourself.

Guys strive to have joy. You are all God's children.

17, 18, 19